HARDWICK HALL

Mark Girouard

THE NATIONAL TRUST

The principal part of the text of this guide was written in
1976 by Mark Girouard. He has updated and revised his
text in consultation with David Durant, and the Trust is
very grateful to them both. The chapter on the park, estate
and garden draws heavily on a survey carried out under the
auspices of the Manpower Services Commission, and in
particular the contribution of Philip Heath, archivist to the
survey, who has also kindly checked the chapter.
Additional notes on the pictures were provided by Alastair
Laing, the National Trust's Pictures Adviser, and on the
garden by Anthony Lord, the National Trust's Gardens
Adviser for Hardwick.

Margaret Willes, *Publisher*

First published in Great Britain in 1989 by the National Trust
Reprinted 1992
Copyright for Chapters 1, 2, 3, 4 and 5 ©1989 Mark Girouard
Copyright for Chapters 6 and 7 ©1989 The National Trust
ISBN 0 7078 0098 6

Photographs: British Library page 85; Chatsworth page 18
(above); Country Life page 42; Courtauld pages 7 (below), 9, 38
(right & left), 39, 66; Brian Delf page 14; Department of the
Environment page 13; Paul Mellon Foundation for British Art
pages 63, 71; National Trust pages 10, 16, 17 (above), 22, 23, 30,
32, 36, 52, 57, 59, 66, 69 (above), 70, 85, 92; National Trust
Photographic Library/John Bethell pages 26 (above & below), 27
(above & below), 28 (above & below), 51 (below), 54, 75, 79,
(above & below); NTPL/Graham Challifour pages 19, 31, 33, 34,
35, 41, 72, 74, 76; NTPL/Country Life page 25; NTPL/Hawkley
Studios pages 5, 6, 7 (above); NTPL/Angelo Hornak pages 43
(above & below), 61; NTPL/Gordon Robertson page 46; NTPL/
Jeremy Whitaker pages 51 (above), 55; NTPL/Mike Williams
pages 12, 18 (below), 21 (above & below), 24, 40, 47, 50, 56, 57,
81, 88, 90, 91 (above & below), 93; RIBA page 17 (below);
Sheffield City Libraries page 8; University of Nottingham page
83; Victoria & Albert Museum page 69 (below); front cover:
NTPL/Rupert Truman; back cover: NTPL/Angelo Hornak.

Designed by James Shurmer

Phototypeset in Monotype Lasercomp Bembo Series 270
by Southern Positives and Negatives (SPAN), Lingfield, Surrey (8549)

Colour reproduction by Acculith 76, Barnet, Hertfordshire

Printed in Italy by Amilcare Pizzi s.p.a., Italy for
The National Trust, 36 Queen Anne's Gate, London SW1H 9AS

CONTENTS

CHAPTER ONE
BESS OF HARDWICK

'A woman of masculine understanding and conduct, proud, furious, selfish and unfeeling. She was a builder, a buyer and seller of estates, a moneylender, a farmer and a merchant of lead, coals and timber; when disengaged from those employments, she intrigued alternately with Elizabeth and Mary, always to the prejudice and terror of her husband.'
Edmund Lodge, *Illustrations of British History*, 1790

Bess of Hardwick's nickname ties her securely to the house she built. So do her initials, with which she decorated its skyline, and her coat of arms, which she scattered profusely over its interiors. There is probably no other house in England which is so closely connected in popular imagination with one person. And she was a person to be reckoned with.

She was born at Hardwick in 1527, one of a family of four girls and a boy. The Hardwicks were minor gentry who had been established at Hardwick for at least six generations. They owned a few hundred acres and lived in a small manor house on the site of Hardwick Old Hall. Bess's father died in 1528, leaving each of his daughters £26 13s 4d. By the 1540s she had gone into service in the household of a neighbouring great Derbyshire family, that of Sir John and Lady Zouche of Codnor Castle.

To be a gentlewoman or upper servant in a big household was an accepted course for the children of the Tudor gentry. It was a form of practical education and a useful step towards marriage. In about 1543 Bess married her cousin Robert Barlow, heir of a Derbyshire gentry family slightly more prosperous than the Hardwicks. The circumstances of the marriage are somewhat mysterious. She is said to have looked after him when he was sick in the Zouche house in London, where he was probably also a member of the household. He died a few months after the marriage, 'before they were bedded' according to one account. Contrary to

legend he did not leave her all his property. She received the customary widow's jointure, probably of a third of his income. By 1588 this amounted to £66 a year, a comfortable little sum by contemporary money values, but certainly not a fortune. As a childless widow she probably continued to serve in great households, and may have become one of the gentlewomen of the Marchioness of Dorset, the mother of Lady Jane Grey. This would explain why her second marriage, to Sir William Cavendish, took place in the Grey family chapel at Bradgate Manor in Leicestershire. It would also explain where she learnt her bold Renaissance handwriting, which, although somewhat running to seed in her old age, contrasts strikingly in her account books with the convoluted Gothic script of her servants.

Her second marriage, which took place in 1547, brought her a notable increase in status. Sir William Cavendish was an elderly, distinguished, and extremely rich government servant, already twice married, with two surviving daughters but no son. He was a typical example of the new men who made their fortune under the Tudors. He had been one of the commissioners for the Dissolution of the Monasteries and in 1546 had bought the lucrative office of Treasurer of the Chamber. In the course of his career he had picked up considerable property, widely scattered over five counties. According to the Duchess of Newcastle (who married Bess's grandson in the mid seventeenth century) 'being somewhat advanced in years, he married her chiefly for her beauty'. To please his new wife he sold all his existing property and bought new property in Derbyshire and Nottinghamshire. Among his purchases were the house and estate of Chatsworth, which he bought in 1549. Up till 1547 these had belonged to Francis Leche, who was both Bess of Hardwick's step-brother and brother-in-law. The Cavendishes pulled down the existing house and

Elizabeth Hardwick, Countess of Shrewsbury. This portrait (9), hanging in the Long Gallery, was painted in the 1590s during her last widowhood

started to build a new one, on the site of the Chatsworth of today.

Bess's Cavendish marriage was not the longest lasting of her marriages but it was much the most successful and the only one which produced children – eight children, of whom three sons and three daughters survived infancy. Her eldest son Henry had no legitimate children (though described by a contemporary as 'the common bull to all Derbyshire and Staffordshire'); from her second son William descended the Cavendishes, Dukes of Devonshire, of Chatsworth and Hardwick, and from her third son Charles, the Cavendishes, Dukes of Newcastle, and Cavendish-Bentincks, Dukes of Portland, of Welbeck and Bolsover. The foundations of these dukedoms were laid by Bess.

With her second marriage she emerged from obscurity and the main aspects of her character became clear. She was capable, managing, acquisitive, a businesswoman, a money maker, a land-amasser, a builder of great houses, an in-

Sir William Cavendish, Bess's second husband, whom she married in 1547 (7). From their marriage the great Cavendish dynasties were derived

defatigable collector of the trappings of wealth and power, and inordinately ambitious, both for herself and her children. She was neither cultured nor religious. She was immensely tough, but it would be a mistake to think of her as either cold or calculating. She was capricious, rash, emotional, fond of intrigue and gossip, easily moved to tears, the best of company when things were going her way and spitting with spite and fury when crossed. Her amazing vitality carried her unflaggingly through her four marriages and widowhood to her death in her eighties, immensely rich and still formidable. Her unrelenting acquisition of property and worldly goods, especially of property in the countryside of her birth, and if possible connected with her family and relatives, suggests the ambition of a local girl to demonstrate that the dim squire's daughter had made good in a sensational way.

William Cavendish died in 1557, leaving her with a life interest in Chatsworth and in a substantial proportion of his property. Two years later she was married again, to a rich West Country landowner, Sir William St Loe. Like William Cavendish he had already been twice married and had daughters. Socially the marriage was yet another step up for Bess, for the St Loes were an older and better-established family than the Cavendishes, and Sir William held the post of Captain of the Guard and Butler of the Royal Household and was a favourite courtier of the Queen's. The marriage only lasted five years; he died in the winter of 1564–65, leaving much of his property outright to Bess, to the indignation of his family. She was on the marriage market again and now a formidable prize. There was much gossip as to whom she would marry next. Her catch, in the end, was a sensational one. In 1567 she married George Talbot, 6th Earl of Shrewsbury, a widower with six children. He was 40, head of one of the oldest, grandest, and richest families in England. By the side of his formidable wife he tends to seem rather a colourless character, but it would be a mistake to under-rate him. He used his inherited wealth as a basis on which he became perhaps the biggest tycoon in England. He was a farmer on an enormous scale, an exploiter of coal mines and glassworks, an ironmaster and shipowner with interests in lead and steel. The main part of his

Although inscribed as a portrait of Queen Mary, this is very probably of Bess of Hardwick, and the only portrait to show her in her prime and beauty

enormous properties was in the Midlands, like those of his new wife. To some extent their marriage can be seen as the merging of two companies. The deal was clinched by a triple marriage; not only did Lord Shrewsbury marry Bess, but his second son married her daughter Mary, and his daughter married her eldest son Henry.

Within two years Lord Shrewsbury was saddled with an important but unenviable assignment. Early in 1569 he was given the custody of Mary, Queen of Scots, who had fled across the border to England in May 1568. He remained her custodian until 1584. She moved between his many houses: Tutbury Castle, Sheffield Castle, Sheffield Manor, Wingfield Manor, Worksop Manor, his lodge at Buxton and his wife's house at Chatsworth. In spite of later legend there is no evidence or likelihood that she was ever at Hardwick.

In 1574 Bess, probably on the spur of the moment, compromised her daughter Elizabeth with Charles Stewart, the brother of Mary, Queen of Scots' ex-husband Lord Darnley. A hurried marriage was arranged between them. Any child of Charles Stuart had a claim to the succession after the death of Elizabeth. The chance of having descendants on the English throne was too tempting for Bess to ignore, but in the long run the marriage brought her nothing but trouble. Queen Elizabeth was justifiably furious, and Charles Stuart's mother spent the winter of 1574–75 imprisoned in the Tower of London. A daughter, Arabella Stuart, born in 1575, was the only child of the marriage; both parents died within a few years leaving Bess as Arabella's guardian.

The Stuart marriage took place without Lord Shrewsbury's knowledge or approval, and it must have seemed to him that his wife was risking his good relations with the Queen for the sake of her own family. Their marriage began to run into

George Talbot, 6th Earl of Shrewsbury, Bess's fourth and last husband (5). At the time of their marriage he was 40, head of one of the richest and oldest families in England

trouble. Another subject of contention was Chatsworth, which Bess was now remodelling on a magnificent scale, and which her husband thought took up a disproportionate amount of her time and interest, and his own money. But probably the main source of strain was Mary, Queen of Scots, who inevitably became a centre of intrigue on a European scale, so that the Shrewsburys lived in a state of constant tension. They had their first serious row in 1577. By 1583 Bess and her sons were spreading rumours (probably without foundation) that Lord Shrewsbury and Mary were having an affair. In 1584 the marriage broke down completely, and, in spite of constant efforts by Queen Elizabeth and the Privy Council, it was never properly patched up.

The collapse of the marriage had important consequences for Hardwick. In about 1583 Bess bought the house and property from her brother James, who had been heavily in debt for many years. When the quarrel between her and her husband broke out one of the bones of contention was Chatsworth, which Lord Shrewsbury claimed belonged to him under the terms of their marriage settlement, and attempted to occupy by force. It remained a subject of dispute for several years, and although Shrewsbury was ordered by the Privy Council to allow her one of his own houses to live

Detail from a page of Bess of Hardwick's accounts in her own hand, listing the contents of her jewel coffer in 1593

in, he made life as difficult as possible for her. Bess accordingly concentrated on her own undisputed property at Hardwick and between about 1585 and 1590 replaced the old house with what is now known as Hardwick Old Hall.

Lord Shrewsbury died in 1590. For some years he had been living with his mistress in a small house outside Sheffield. Bess now recovered complete control of all her lands with a very large widow's jointure in addition. She was in her early sixties, and one of the richest people in England. Immediately after her husband's death, or possibly even a few weeks before it, she laid out the foundations of a new, larger and grander house a few yards away from the still uncompleted Hardwick Old Hall. Hardwick, rather than Chatsworth, became her principal home, perhaps because it was her own property and the place where she had been born, whereas she only had a life interest in Chatsworth. After her death it would go to her eldest son Henry, who had taken her husband's side in the quarrel, and whom she heartily disliked; Hardwick, on the other hand, was destined for her favourite son, William.

The next thirteen years were spent in building and furnishing Hardwick, in running her properties, making money, buying even more land for herself and her sons, and coping with the increasing problem of Arabella. The pretty bright-eyed baby shown in the portrait in the drawing room at Hardwick had grown into a spoilt and lively girl who was well aware that many people were betting on her chances of being the next queen of England. She became the centre of numerous intrigues, mostly concerned with marrying her to various important people. Queen Elizabeth played her usual game of refusing to commit herself; she checkmated all marriage plans and showed no signs of declaring Arabella or anyone else her heir. Arabella paid occasional visits to court, but mostly she was made to live safely out of the way at Hardwick. Her grandmother was by now too old to plot; at any rate she dutifully did what the Queen wanted, and kept Arabella under strict supervision. The situation dragged on until Arabella was in her late twenties and still unmarried; not unnaturally she grew to hate her grandmother, became increasingly in-

William Cavendish, second son of Bess and William Cavendish (10). Favoured above his elder brother, Henry, he inherited Hardwick from his mother

volved in intrigue, and finally seems to have gone a little mad. Matters came to a head in 1603, a year of plots, rows and mounting tension at Hardwick, with Privy Councillors passing to and fro, Arabella in hysterics and Henry Cavendish involved in an intrigue to abduct her and possibly attempt to proclaim her queen. But it all came to nothing; Elizabeth died, declaring James I her heir on her deathbed; James took a fancy to Arabella, brought her to London and showered favours on her. She only returned to Hardwick for one short visit in 1605; in 1610 she made a surreptitious marriage to the Earl of Hertford, the most dangerous of possible claimants to the throne, and was sent to the Tower of London, where she died in 1615.

At Hardwick, after Arabella had left, peace returned to the ancient Countess for the remaining five years of her life. She died on 13 February 1608, with 'the blessing of sense and memory to the last'. Legends later grew up of a prophecy foretelling that she would never die while she was building, and of the famously fierce winter of 1607–8 putting a stop to her building activities in spite of boiling ale instead of water being used to melt the mortar. Unfortunately there is no evidence of any building activity in the last years of her life: Hardwick was finished and so was her smaller house at Oldcotes, which she built for her son William and which has been demolished. But we do know from contem-porary sources that the amazing sum of £1584 7s 9d (multiply at least by twenty to get the modern equivalent) was paid for mourning cloth to cele-brate her death.

Bess was buried in great state in the church of All Hallows, Derby, now the cathedral. The epitaph on her tomb celebrated her as the 'aedificatrix' of Chatsworth, Hardwick and Oldcotes.

Lady Arabella Stuart, Bess's troublesome granddaughter (83). The only child of the marriage of Elizabeth Cavendish, Bess's second daughter, and Charles Stewart, Earl of Lennox. She had a claim to the English throne through her father. This delightful portrait, now in the Drawing Room, was painted when she was nearly two years old

FAMILY TREE OF HARDWICK AND CAVENDISH

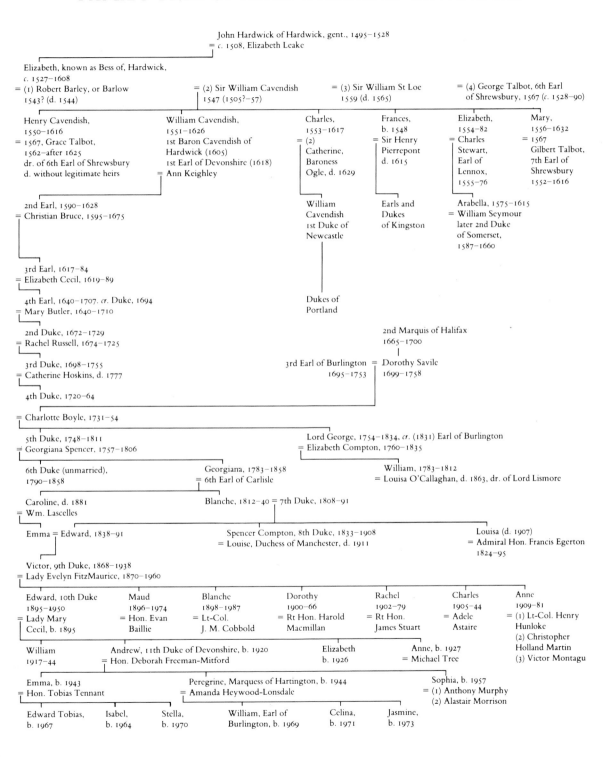

John Hardwick of Hardwick, gent., 1495–1528
= c. 1508, Elizabeth Leake

Elizabeth, known as Bess of, Hardwick,
c. 1527–1608
= (1) Robert Barley, or Barlow   = (2) Sir William Cavendish   = (3) Sir William St Loe   = (4) George Talbot, 6th Earl
1543? (d. 1544)   1547 (1505?–57)   1559 (d. 1565)   of Shrewsbury, 1567 (c. 1528–90)

Henry Cavendish,   William Cavendish,   Charles,   Frances,   Elizabeth,   Mary,
1550–1616   1551–1626   1553–1617   b. 1548   1554–82   1556–1632
= 1567, Grace Talbot,   1st Baron Cavendish of   = (2)   = Sir Henry   = Charles   = 1567
1562–after 1625   Hardwick (1605)   Catherine,   Pierrepont   Stewart,   Gilbert Talbot,
dr. of 6th Earl of Shrewsbury   1st Earl of Devonshire (1618)   Baroness   d. 1615   Earl of   7th Earl of
d. without legitimate heirs   = Ann Keighley   Ogle, d. 1629   Lennox,   Shrewsbury
            1555–76   1552–1616

2nd Earl, 1590–1628   William   Earls and   Arabella, 1575–1615
= Christian Bruce, 1595–1675   Cavendish   Dukes   = William Seymour
   1st Duke of   of Kingston   later 2nd Duke
   Newcastle   of Somerset,
         1587–1660

3rd Earl, 1617–84
= Elizabeth Cecil, 1619–89

4th Earl, 1640–1707. cr. Duke, 1694   Dukes of
= Mary Butler, 1640–1710   Portland

2nd Duke, 1672–1729   2nd Marquis of Halifax
= Rachel Russell, 1674–1725   1665–1700

3rd Duke, 1698–1755   3rd Earl of Burlington   =   Dorothy Savile
= Catherine Hoskins, d. 1777   1695–1753   1699–1758

4th Duke, 1720–64
= Charlotte Boyle, 1731–54

5th Duke, 1748–1811   Lord George, 1754–1834, cr. (1831) Earl of Burlington
= Georgiana Spencer, 1757–1806   = Elizabeth Compton, 1760–1835

6th Duke (unmarried),   Georgiana, 1783–1858   William, 1783–1812
1790–1858   = 6th Earl of Carlisle   = Louisa O'Callaghan, d. 1863, dr. of Lord Lismore

Caroline, d. 1881   Blanche, 1812–40 = 7th Duke, 1808–91
= Wm. Lascelles

Emma = Edward, 1838–91   Spencer Compton, 8th Duke, 1833–1908   Louisa (d. 1907)
   = Louise, Duchess of Manchester, d. 1911   = Admiral Hon. Francis Egerton
      1824–95

Victor, 9th Duke, 1868–1938
= Lady Evelyn FitzMaurice, 1870–1960

Edward, 10th Duke	Maud	Blanche	Dorothy	Rachel	Charles	Anne
1895–1950	1896–1974	1898–1987	1900–66	1902–79	1905–44	1909–81
= Lady Mary	= Hon. Evan	= Lt-Col.	= Rt Hon. Harold	= Rt Hon.	= Adele	= (1) Lt-Col. Henry
Cecil, b. 1895	Baillie	J. M. Cobbold	Macmillan	James Stuart	Astaire	Hunloke
						(2) Christopher

William   Andrew, 11th Duke of Devonshire, b. 1920   Elizabeth   Anne, b. 1927   Holland Martin
1917–44   = Hon. Deborah Freeman-Mitford   b. 1926   = Michael Tree   (3) Victor Montagu

Emma, b. 1943   Peregrine, Marquess of Hartington, b. 1944   Sophia, b. 1957
= Hon. Tobias Tennant   = Amanda Heywood-Lonsdale   = (1) Anthony Murphy
      (2) Alastair Morrison

Edward Tobias,	Isabel,	Stella,	William, Earl of	Celina,	Jasmine,
b. 1967	b. 1964	b. 1970	Burlington, b. 1969	b. 1971	b. 1973

CHAPTER TWO

THE BUILDING OF HARDWICK

'Higher yet in the very East frontier of this county, upon a rough and a craggie soile standeth Hardwic, which gave name to a family in which possessed the same: out of which descended Lady Elizabeth, Countess of Shrewsbury, who beganne to build there two goodly houses joining in a maner one to the other, which by reason of their lofty situation shew themselves, a farre off to be seene, and yeeld a very goodly prospect.'
William Camden, *Britannia*, 1610

Hardwick is fortunate in that the greater part of its building accounts have survived. They cover the period from 1587, when work on the Old Hall was already in course, until 1599, when work on the New Hall was approaching completion. In addition, two accounts books for the years 1591–98 and 1598–1601 have occasional references to building, besides, of course, giving fascinating information about life at Hardwick. An inventory of 1601 gives the original use of the rooms.

To many visitors to Hardwick, it is a matter of amazement to find two such large houses existing side by side, especially when they learn that both houses were more or less fully furnished and in use at the same time; Hardwick Old Hall only became ruinous in the eighteenth century. When Bess started to remodel the Old Hall in about 1585 her husband was still alive and she did not have the means to embark on anything as magnificent as the New Hall. As she and her husband were of an age there was no especial likelihood that she would survive him.

The central portion of Hardwick Old Hall is irregular and gabled, perhaps representing in much altered form the house that already existed when Bess took up residence. At either end she added two substantial and roughly balancing wings, with level balustraded parapets. At the top of each wing above three storeys of comparatively low rooms was a series of immense and lofty state rooms, lit by towering windows. One wing has a tower six storeys high, the other shallow projecting bays running all the way up. Possibly as a result of the haphazard way the

A seventeenth-century drawing of the Old and New Halls at Hardwick. To the right stands the Old Hall with its two wings topped by balustraded parapets. The long windows in the right-hand wing show the position of one of the great chambers. The drawing comes from a scrapbook at Audley End in Essex

(*Left*) The entrance front of Hardwick Hall

13

house was built, it has the unique feature of two full-scale great chambers, the Hill Great Chamber and the Forest Great Chamber, at the west and east ends of the house. But perhaps the most revolutionary feature is the great hall, two storeys high, going across the centre of the house, in a position radically different from the conventional medieval one. Bess was to use this feature again to great effect.

Shrewsbury's death in 1590 improved Bess's financial situation and encouraged her to build the New Hall. But she continued to live in the Old Hall until the New Hall was ready for occupation in 1597; in fact the Old Hall was still being finished while the new one was being built. Thereafter it was used to provide a useful supply of extra accommodation for both servants and guests. The size of the New Hall must always have been calculated with this in mind for, large though it is, it was by no means large by comparison with other great Elizabethan houses such as Burghley, Holdenby or, for that matter, Chatsworth. On the other hand, the scale and splendour of the state apartment on the second floor suggests that it was specifically built in the hope of royal visits of a future Queen Arabella.

Both houses were built of the same stone, quarried just down the hill, and in many cases the same craftsmen worked on both of them, but the results were very different. The Old Hall looks as if it had been designed as it went along; the New Hall is splendidly all of a piece. The difference reflects the more settled and prosperous conditions under which the New Hall was started, but also the fact that a new mind had got to work on its design. There is little doubt that its plan was provided by Robert Smythson (c.1535–1614), one of the most original of Elizabethan architects.

The term architect is somewhat misleading, however, for the concept of an architect was only in its embryonic stages in Elizabethan England. Robert Smythson was trained as a stonemason. By the 1560s he had become a master-mason, travelling round England with a gang of masons working under him. As such he was brought from London to Wiltshire in 1568 to assist in the rebuilding of Sir John Thynne's house at Longleat. He worked there on and off for twelve years, carved much of the external detail himself and had a considerable

influence on its design. In 1580 he moved on to Wollaton Hall in Nottinghamshire where he was surveyor rather than master-mason, both designing the house and superintending its erection; by now he had stopped working as a mason. He settled at Wollaton and remained there until his death in 1614, when he was described on his monument in the church as 'architect and surveyour unto the most worthy house of Wollaton and divers others of great account'.

Among those 'divers others' was Worksop Manor in Nottinghamshire, which was remodelled to his design around 1585 for Bess's husband the Earl of Shrewsbury. Bess may have had a hand in the first stages of its rebuilding, but as it went up her marriage finally exploded. Fear of upsetting a powerful patron may, as a result, have made Smythson unwilling to work for Bess at Hardwick until after her husband's death.

The evidence that he provided designs for the new house at Hardwick is not absolutely conclusive, but it is extremely strong. The account book which may have contained payments for them has disappeared, but the general account book for 1597, the year in which the house was finished, records a gift on 27 March of £1 to 'Mr. Smythson the surveyour' and 10s to his son. Among his drawings, now belonging to the RIBA in London, is a plan unmistakably connected with Hardwick, though with minor variations. He and his son John subsequently did work for Bess's son Charles, including the design (by John) of Bolsover Castle, a few miles up the M1 from Hardwick. And stylistically Hardwick is a natural development from Longleat, Wollaton and, especially, Worksop. On the other hand there is no evidence or likelihood that Smythson closely supervised the building of Hardwick. It was probably a case, as often happened with Elizabethan houses, of a 'surveyor' providing plans and elevations, leaving the detailing to the workmen on the spot, who made alterations to suit their own convenience or as dictated by the client while work was in progress.

In Hardwick three of the most notable characteristics of the Elizabethans and their architecture reach culminating expression: their enthusiasm for symmetry, for what were called at the time 'devices', and for huge expanses of glass. Symmetry applied to domestic (as opposed to ecclesiastical) architecture was essentially a Tudor innovation and one can still sense at houses like Hardwick and Montacute the delight with which their builders balanced tower against tower and lined up the porter's lodge with the front door, between symmetrical pavilions. But at Hardwick not only the entrance front is symmetrical; the house is symmetrical on all four sides and its basic scheme of a rectangle surrounded by six towers, two to each long and one to each short side, is simple as an idea but ingeniously complex in its results, for the towers assume an endless variety of groupings according to the angle from which they are looked at. Examples of this type of ingenuity

were called 'devices' by the Elizabethans. They used the term over a wide range to cover, for instance, buildings of complex or original plan, acrostic or riddle poems, and the jewels incorporating a symbolic picture and matching motto which courtiers devised to sum up their approach to life and wore when jousting in front of the Queen.

Various means were used to obtain complete all-round symmetry at Hardwick, and yet provide the rooms of all shapes and sizes that were needed. A few windows are completely false and have chimneypieces behind them. In a number of cases what seems to be one window on the exterior conceals two storeys; four low-ceilinged bedrooms, for instance, are concealed between the top lights of the

The Hill Great Chamber of the Old Hall, so called because it stands on the hill side of the house

(*Far right, above*) Worksop Manor, Nottinghamshire, remodelled and enlarged for the 6th Earl of Shrewsbury by Robert Smythson *c*.1585

(*Far right, below*) A design by Robert Smythson in the style of Hardwick, now in the RIBA in London

(*Above*) Tudor Chatsworth, built by Sir William Cavendish and Bess from 1549, and now encased by the seventeenth-century baroque house of their descendants. The view is from a needlework panel at Chatsworth

(*Below*) 'Hardwick Hall, more glass than wall'. One of the corner towers, topped by Bess's initials and countess's coronet

six upper left-hand windows on the entrance façade. More important, the Hall goes through the middle of the house instead of running along the entrance front; the latter was the normal Elizabethan arrangement, inherited from the Middle Ages, but was difficult to combine with a symmetrical façade, particularly if the hall rose through two storeys. The Hardwick arrangement had already been adapted in the Old Hall and was to be imitated in a number of later houses, such as Charlton Hall near Greenwich.

'Hardwick Hall, more glass than wall' has become a familiar jingle. Other Elizabethan houses, including Smythson's Longleat, Wollaton and Worksop, had huge windows, but Hardwick went further than any of them. Nearly all the chimney flues are carried up through the internal walls leaving the external façades available for as much glass as could be provided with structural safety. These great windows were pursued by the Elizabethans and Jacobeans as status symbols (for glass was very expensive) regardless of comfort; as Francis Bacon wrote in his Essays 'You shall have sometimes fair houses so full of glass, that one cannot tell where to become to be out of the sun or cold'. Until the introduction of central heating Hardwick, on its hill top, was bitterly cold in winter.

One of the most unusual features of both the Old and New Halls at Hardwick was the great hall going through the middle of the house rather than along the entrance front. This view of the hall at Hardwick is shown through the stone entrance screen

The impressiveness of Hardwick's glass façades is much increased by their height. High buildings seem to have appealed to Bess; Chatsworth, Worksop and Hardwick Old Hall were all unusually high buildings for their date. One reason for this was that they were a storey higher than was normal, for Bess liked to have her high-ceilinged state rooms up on the second floor, instead of on the first, as was usual at the time. And at Hardwick the house is made higher still by its six great turrets. The accounts show that these were altered in the course of building operations to increase their height, no doubt to obtain an even more impressive effect.

Other alterations were made as the building went up. The loggias were originally intended to run right round the building instead of only between the towers on the two main fronts; one can still see the line of rough stone at the corners where their roofs would have been tied in, but these portions were never built, probably because it was felt that they would make the rooms behind them too dark. The two staircases were probably originally intended to rise straight up through the house from their starting point at either side of the Hall. This would have made the present planning of the top floor impossible, for both would have come up in the middle of what is now the Long Gallery. At some stage, possibly even while the house was being built, the present arrangement was adopted, by which both staircases gradually work their way to the turrets at either end of the house. The result is unique to Hardwick and their long processional route through the middle of the house, especially that of the main staircase, with constantly changing views and contrasts of light and shade, is one of the most memorable features of the house.

Elizabethan houses such as Hardwick reflect a miscellany of stylistic influences; the result is often clumsy or indigestible, but not always so, and Hardwick is a memorable example of a mixture that works. The symmetry of its plan and layout and its two loggias show the influence of the Renaissance; its towers and huge grids of glass derive from Perpendicular Gothic; its detail came from a number of sources, but much the strongest influence is the Mannerist architecture of the Low Countries, as popularised in England through the pattern books published at Antwerp by Vredeman de Vries and other architects. Among the most prominent features of this Flemish style was its use of obelisks and the motif known as strap work and these are omnipresent at Hardwick, modelled in stone, marble or plaster as overmantels throughout the two houses and crowning its silhouette on towers, lodges, and courtyard walls.

Robert Smythson is unlikely to have had much to do with this detail. It was probably designed by the craftsmen working on the house, though in many cases they will have derived their designs from books or engravings, either belonging to them or supplied by Bess or someone in her circle. The chimneypieces in the Long Gallery and Bess's Withdrawing Chamber, for instance, seem to derive, with considerable modifications, from designs in Serlio's *Architecture*; the plasterwork figures of Summer and of Venus chastising Cupid in the High Great Chamber, and of the four Elements on overmantels in the Old Hall, come from engravings by the elder Crispin van der Passe from designs by Martin de Vos. Actual engravings by Peter de Coster of Antwerp are pasted onto the panelling in the High Great Chamber as decoration.

A possible route by which engravings of this type came to Hardwick is through one of the craftsmen working there, the painter John Ballechouse. His name suggests a Low Countries origin and was so indigestible to Derbyshire clerks that he is normally referred to in the accounts as John Painter. He first appears working for Bess at Chatsworth in 1578 and remained with her until her death, after which he was in charge of the mysterious building or decorating operations carried out at Hardwick by her son. In Bess's lifetime he was almost certainly responsible for the painted frieze in the Long Gallery, for the stencils of arabesques or strap work which cover much of the panelling, and probably for the painted cloths at present in the Chapel.

Many of the craftsmen at Hardwick had worked with each other before, either at Chatsworth or under Smythson at Wollaton. The greater part of the masonry was contracted for by John and Christopher Rodes, who had been the main contractors at Wollaton. Among other masons William Griffin carved the Hall screen, and one of the stone

Classical motifs in the High Great Chamber. (*Above*) Summer or Venus chastising Cupid on the plasterwork frieze. These figures are devices from engravings by Crispin van der Passe from designs by Martin de Vos. (*Below*) Actual engravings by Peter Coster of Antwerp, pasted onto the panelling

Alabaster and blackstone chimneypiece and door surrounds in the Best Bedchamber, now the Green Velvet Room. These were erected by Thomas Accres in 1599

surrounds on the Chapel landing (the latter jointly with James Adams). Two other masons, Henry Nayll and Richard Mallory, carved another of the Chapel landing doors and assisted Thomas Accres with the elaborate alabaster and blackstone decoration surrounding the door and chimneypiece in the Best Bedchamber. Accres, who had previously worked both at Chatsworth and Wollaton, was an important member of the Hardwick team, and the general payments to him in the accounts may cover chimneypieces in stone, alabaster or blackstone throughout the house; but payments for specific chimneypieces or plasterwork are regrettably absent from the accounts. The more elaborate plasterwork was probably modelled by Abraham Smith, who had been at Chatsworth. Ballechouse, Accres and Smith remained full-time employees of Bess up till her death, each being paid with a quarterly wage and the free lease of a farm.

Stone, as already mentioned, came from the quarry down the hill, wood mostly from Bess's woods, and glass probably from her glassworks at Wingfield. Blackstone came from her quarries at Ashford in Derbyshire and was cut at a sawmill constructed by Thomas Accres in 1595 and referred

to in the accounts as the 'engine'. Alabaster came from Creswell a few miles north of the house. Iron came fom her ironworks at Wingfield, lead from lead workings at Winster, Aldwark and Bonsall, which Bess had handed over to her son William. So Hardwick was to a large extent a local product, built from local materials mostly drawn from Bess's own property and by local craftsmen or craftsmen who had been working for her for many years. In the same way many of the embroideries were worked either by Bess and her ladies or by professional embroiderers on her staff. Tapestries and plate, on the other hand, had to be bought in London or elsewhere; the tapestries largely survive, the Aladdin's cave of sumptuous plate that covers page after page of the inventory has all vanished and was probably sold or melted down in the seventeenth century. No furniture appears in the Hardwick accounts, apart from a few tables and forms run up in the house by her own joiners; probably much furniture was brought over from Chatsworth, along with embroideries, hangings, pictures and plate, for Chatsworth was thoroughly plundered to benefit Hardwick as Bess lived more and more there.

CHAPTER THREE

THE HARDWICK EMBROIDERIES

Although the tapestries, pictures and furniture at Hardwick each form an interesting collection, its unique feature is its great wealth of sixteenth- and early seventeenth-century embroideries; no other house in Europe can approach its richness and although some museums have larger collections they lack the unifying factor of all having been made for, and in most cases by, one household. The bulk of the embroideries was executed between about 1570 and 1640; the earlier ones in this period were made for Chatsworth and brought over by Bess in the 1590s to furnish her new house at Hardwick, the later ones date from the time of Christian, Countess of Devonshire, the wife of Bess's grandson, the 2nd Earl.

Bess probably always had one or more full-time

Penelope, one of Bess's favourite heroines, flanked by Perserverance and Patience. The wall hanging forms part of the scenes of famous and worthy heroines created in the 1570s, now to be found in the Entrance Hall

embroiderers on her staff. In 1598 'Webb the imbroderer' was paid 18s 4d a quarter, a wage which put him lower on the scale than the porter, butler or blacksmith and higher than the laundress and glazier. An entry in the accounts for 1591 shows that an embroiderer had a chamber and inner chamber allotted to him in the Old Hall. According to Bess's own evidence the famous Hardwick wall hangings of classical matrons and accompanying virtues were made at Chatsworth by her grooms, women, and 'some boys she kept', with the assistance of a professional embroiderer. Judging by the quality and scale of the work this professional must have been of higher standing than the ill-paid Webb, who could, perhaps, also be described as a 'boy she kept'. It is likely that many of the smaller embroideries were the work of Bess herself and her gentlewomen, perhaps with the aid of a professional to set out the design. On the other hand the accounts of Christian, Countess of Devonshire, record payment for the applied work on the stools and chairs in the High Great Chamber to a professional embroiderer called George Savage (who may, however, only have been applying embroideries worked by the Countess and her ladies); and the two cushion covers showing the Judgement of Solomon and Sacrifice of Isaac, now in the Hall, are from a

professional workshop and must have come to Bess by gift or purchase. But there is little doubt that the major part of the embroideries was executed at Chatsworth or Hardwick. In spite of widespread belief to the contrary there is nothing that can be positively attributed to Mary, Queen of Scots, except for two panels which may only have come to Hardwick in the nineteenth century.

Today most of the embroideries not in store or in the exhibition in the Schoolroom are displayed framed or as screens, but originally they served many purposes, especially as wall or bed hangings, table carpets and cushion covers. A number of different techniques was used. The most impressive of these is the use of applied work, especially in the form of velvets and patterned silks cut out and made into pictorial wall hangings. The velvets and silks used are mostly Italian fifteenth- and sixteenth-century weavings, and some certainly came from church vestments; in 1557 Sir William Cavendish bought copes originating from the dissolved religious house at Lilleshall in Shropshire, and more vestments came through Sir William St Loe in the 1560s. Only the woven silks and velvets were cut up; the embroidered 'orphreys' (ornamental borders) and hoods were put aside and still survive at Hardwick made up into panels described

A tent-stitch cushion cover depicting an Old Testament scene, The Sacrifice of Isaac, in the style of a professional workshop, probably French. This cover is now displayed in a frame in the Entrance Hall

Mahomet lying at the feet of Faith, a detail from one of the wall hangings in the Entrance Hall depicting virtues with historic characters which embodied their contrary vices. The hangings, from a patchwork of pieces of material including fragments cut out of medieval copes, were made in the 1570s

Two pieces of applied work of the late sixteenth century.

(*Above*) a valance decorated with pieces of velvet and silk to create a fisherman surrounded by animals and plants.

(*Below*) strapwork and interlacing patterns on plain velvet, with birds painted onto velvet roundels

A red velvet cushion cover decorated with strapwork made up of strips of cloth of silver, flowers and leaves

A tent-stitch cushion cover depicting the Fall of Phaeton. Now displayed in the Dining Room

in the 1601 inventory and elsewhere as 'church work'.

The inventory refers to 'nyne payres of beames for imbroiderers' in the wardrobe on the second floor of the New Hall. These 'beames' are sometimes also described as 'tents', from the French *tenter*, to stretch, because the canvas on which the embroidery was worked was stretched on them. On them must have been worked in cross-stitch (or 'tent-stitch', as it is sometimes called) many of the cushion covers at Hardwick, all around 40 inches by 20 inches, the maximum size for a handy embroidery frame. Tent-stitch was also used for separate flowers, sprigs, trees etc. for use in applied work. Another very common product of the Hardwick embroiderers were panels of red velvet on which strips of cloth of silver were sewn down to form interlacing quatrefoils and rectangles, edged with gilt cord and filled in with flowers and leaves. This style of ornament was described as 'fret' and continued to be used at Hardwick into the seventeenth century. A much less common technique, examples of which have not survived in any quantity except at Hardwick, was to set out strap work and interlacing patterns on plain velvet, outline them with couched embroidery in silk or velvet, and then paint the velvet in contrasting colours.

The embroideries are profusely decorated with Bess's and other monograms, and the arms, crests and supporters of Hardwick, Cavendish and Talbot, especially the Hardwick stag and eglantine. Motifs other than family and heraldic ones must often have been derived from engraved sources; in a number of cases these have been identified, and are referred to in the description of the individual rooms later on in this guide.

A display of some of the other sixteenth- and early seventeenth-century embroideries that were in the house when it was given to the National Trust in 1956 is in the Schoolroom beyond the main staircase on the ground floor. Its contents are described in a separate booklet.

Bess of Hardwick's monogram and arms frequently appear in embroideries from her collection. (*Above*) a panel of velvet with padded appliqué of cloth of gold and silver shows the Hardwick crest and 'E.S.' (*Below*) a table carpet with the crest within the Order of the Garter

CHAPTER FOUR

LIFE AT HARDWICK

Food and drink consumed at Hardwick during the New Year festivities, 26 December to 1 January, 1668–69.

71	beefs	7	plovers
180	muttons	4	str apples
51	veals	18	geese
1	calfs head	11	partridges
22	tongues	30	woodcocks
1	capon	4	barrels oysters
57	pullets	10	pigs
16	chickens	10	turkeys
98	rabbits	6	brawns
3/4	venison	9	widgeons
32	porks	2	peewits (?)
1	grenfish (?)	10	hogshead small beer
5	carps	2	hogshead strong beer
2	pike	5	hogshead small ale
32	bacons	34	quarts sherry
251	butters	19	quarts celery wine
1500	eggs	30	quarts claret
6	cheeses	30	quarts white wine
22	gallons cream		

Provisions book of the 3rd Earl of Devonshire

Hardwick, like other grand Elizabethan households, was organised like a little court. At the centre was Bess herself and round her radiated three concentric circles: her own immediate family, the upper servants, and the lower servants. The division between upper and lower servants was a crucial one in all big Elizabethan households. The upper servants were more like courtiers than servants in our sense of the word. They were usually the younger sons or daughters of good families, were known as 'Mr' or 'Mrs' and counted as gentlemen and gentlewomen, as opposed to the lower servants who were classed as yeomen. Bess herself had been in such service as a girl and the gentlemen servants at

Hardwick included (until he was sent away in disgrace in 1600) her own nephew, George Knyveton, the son of her half-sister Jane, who lived with her at Hardwick. The gentlemen were employed in running the estate as well as the household, for a separate estate office with its own staff was a much later development. At their head was the steward, normally the chief officer of the household and a person of great importance. But Hardwick was a woman-oriented household and the best paid and probably most influential of the upper servants was Mrs Digby, the chief of Bess's gentlewomen; she was paid three times as much as her husband, who was also in the household. The position of these gentlewomen was not unlike that of the Queen's ladies-in-waiting today; they were Bess's companions and assistants, entertained her guests and helped work the embroideries which are still such a feature of Hardwick.

The upper servants ran the stables, and organised life in the upstairs rooms, but all the heavy work was done by the lower servants. The hall, kitchen, cellars, and offices were run by the cream of the lower servants, the NCOs so to speak, of the household; at their head was the clerk of the kitchen, an important official whose responsibilities ranged far beyond the actual kitchen. Among his subordinates was the yeoman of the buttery, also known as the butler, who was in charge of the buttery and beer cellar, and was a much less important figure in the household than the butlers of the nineteenth and twentieth centuries. A distinctive feature of the work of the lower servants, as opposed to servants in big households two or three centuries later, was that it was the men who did most of the work. In addition to the waiters, the cooks and scullions were all men, and all the cleaning of the house was done by men. The only women among the lower servants were ladies' maids, nurses for the children (if there were any) and laundry maids, and the latter worked outside the house.

As noble Elizabethan households went, that at Hardwick was not especially large. Bess had about thirty indoor servants of both ranks on her payroll. In addition Arabella had her own small staff, and the size of the household would have been increased by at least another ten when Bess's son William kept house with her, as he seems to have done for some of the year. These servants did not live apart in their own little world behind a green baize door, like the Victorian servants for whom an inconspicuous servants' wing was built at Hardwick in the mid nineteenth century. Self-contained servants' wings only became feasible through the invention of bell-pulls, connected by wires running from individual rooms to the long row of bells in the servants' corridor. Before that servants had to be within calling distance. At Hardwick they slept, for instance, all over the place. The upper servants had their own well-furnished rooms, mostly in the Old Hall. The lower servants bedded down more indiscriminately, on landings on the main staircase, outside Bess's bedchamber door, in the scullery, off the pantry and the hall, or in the porter's lodge and the turrets round the entrance court. In addition all the grander bedrooms had their 'pallets', a rolled-up straw mattress which could be pulled out at night for a servant to sleep on in the bedchamber or just outside the door, at hand to protect or serve his master or mistress.

During the daytime the lower servants ate, and when not otherwise employed sat, played cards and gossiped, in the hall. The owners of great Elizabethan houses had long ceased eating in the hall, except on rare occasions. In some households their place at the high table was taken by the upper servants, presided over by the steward, but at Hardwick there was no high table in the hall, and only the lower servants ate there. There would probably have been forty or fifty people in it at a busy period, for the outdoor servants ate there as well, as did visiting servants and Bess's little gang of resident craftsmen who were busy probably up to her death in finishing off the decorations of the house. These included Abraham Smith the plasterer and his son, Thomas Accres the mason and marble cutter with his assistants Laurence Dolphin and Miles Padley, and John Ballechouse the painter with his son James. On feasts and holidays the room

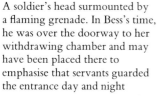

A soldier's head surmounted by a flaming grenade. In Bess's time, he was over the doorway to her withdrawing chamber and may have been placed there to emphasise that servants guarded the entrance day and night

(*Far right*) The great main staircase of Hardwick rising right through the height of the house. The photograph shows the upper half, leading to the High Great Chamber

would almost certainly have been much more crowded; later account books show as many as 300 tenants, friends, servants and others being entertained at one go in and around Christmas and the New Year in the 1660s.

But this animated, companionable and noisy room was also the room through which all visitors, even the most important, had to thread their way, while the usher of the hall shouted 'silence my masters' in an effort to still the noise; all Elizabethan and Jacobean household regulations are full of instructions aimed at keeping down the noise in the hall. It seems strange to us that the servants' hall should also be the entrance hall. But most Elizabethan rooms served two or more purposes even when, as at Hardwick, there was no shortage of space. Dining rooms were also sitting rooms, music rooms and ball rooms. Bedrooms were more

like bedsitting rooms. Although Bess had her own withdrawing room she conducted business and wrote her letters in the inner security of her bedchamber; here, as the inventory shows, she kept her writing table and her books, and stored her papers and her money in a great iron chest and a miscellaneous series of coffers and boxes.

The fact that the functions of rooms were much less differentiated than they were, for instance, in Victorian times, does not mean that life in Hardwick was a haphazard affair. Bess must have lived in an atmosphere of continual ceremony. The arrival of an important guest was a ceremonial event and so was the serving of her food when she ate in state in the High Great Chamber, served by waiters on bended knee. Even the act of sitting down was a ceremony, for in each of the rooms she frequented she had her own special chair, decorated with gold

(*Right*) The High Great Chamber as it appears today and (*above*) an engraving of 1835 from P. Robinson's *New Vitruvius Britannicus* showing the canopy of state erected by the 2nd Earl of Devonshire in position, and the state bed brought from Chatsworth by the 6th Duke and wrongly identified as belonging to Mary Queen of Scots

or silver and with an upholstered footstool, necessary as well as ornamental because of the height of the chair. The house was divided not according to function, with living rooms below and bedrooms above, but according to state; on each floor the rooms grew more ceremonial.

The ceremonial pivot of the house was the High Great Chamber. In all large Elizabethan houses the great chamber had taken the place of pre-eminence held in the Middle Ages by the great hall. As a contemporary set of household regulations put it 'In that place there must be no delay, because it is the place of state, where the lord keepeth his presence, and the eyes of all the best sort of strangers be there lookers on . . . wherefore the gentleman ushers is to take a special care herein for their credit sake and

honour of that place'. The great chamber was always the most sumptuously decorated room in an Elizabethan house. Often, as at Hardwick, the decoration included the royal coat of arms as a demonstration of loyalty. It could be used for receiving and entertaining important guests, for dancing and music, or for performing masques and plays: the Queen's players were at Hardwick in September 1600, and may have performed in the High Great Chamber or Gallery. But the principal use of a great chamber was as the room where dinner and supper were served with great ceremony whenever the lord or lady were 'keeping their state'. A key part of the ceremony was the actual arrival of the food, carried in a formal procession right the way up from the servery by the kitchen, through

The Long Gallery at Hardwick with Lapierre's canopy in the distance

the great hall (where everyone present stood up in its honour) and up the interminable flights of the great staircase to its final destination in the great chamber.

Dinner was normally served at eleven in the morning, supper at five or six. At the end of each meal the family and guests retired to a withdrawing chamber next to the High Great Chamber, while the remains of the meal were cleared away from the latter and it was prepared for possible music or dancing later on. On the other side of the withdrawing chamber was almost always the best bedchamber, where important guests were installed. Great chamber, withdrawing chamber and best bedchamber form the standard ceremonial sequence in all big Elizabethan houses, and Hardwick was no exception. To this was usually added a long gallery, as at Hardwick. The long gallery was another multi-purpose room: it was used as an alternative reception room to the great chamber, for

exercise in wet or cold weather, for the hanging of portraits, and above all, perhaps, as a status symbol.

Hardwick, like both the Old Hall and Chatsworth, had the unusual peculiarity of a second great chamber, known as the Low Great Chamber, on the first floor. This room was probably the equivalent of a dining parlour which was a normal feature on the ground floor of Elizabethan houses; the change of name may have been due to the fact that, because of Bess's idiosyncratic planning, the room is on the first floor, and parlours were always thought of as ground floor rooms. The Low Great Chamber, together with Bess's own withdrawing chamber linked to it by the gallery across the hall, and with her bedchamber and the chambers of William Cavendish and Arabella Stuart beyond it, made up a family and household suite, as opposed to the state suite with its similar sequence of High Great Chamber, Withdrawing Chamber and Best Bedchamber, on the floor above. The Low Great Chamber was used by Bess for eating in on less formal occasions and seems also to have been used as a common-room by the upper servants; Arabella refers, in a letter of March 1603, to a group of them gossiping in it and 'taking the advantage of the fire to warm them by'. The little dining chamber off the Low Great Chamber may either have been used as a completely private dining chamber by Bess or (as the comparatively simple nature of the original furnishings suggests) as a dining room for the upper servants.

The ground floor was occupied by the nurseries, and a few bedchambers, but mainly by the lower half of the hall and chapel, and by the kitchen and offices: the pastry, where bread was baked in great brick-lined ovens; the scullery; the pantry, where the plate, bread and table linen were kept, and which had access to the wine cellar; and the buttery, where beer was served and from which stairs led down to the beer cellars. So the house was approximately divided into a floor for servants, a floor for the family and a floor for state. This hierarchy is exactly expressed on the exterior by the increasing height of the windows.

In 1601 the turrets on the roof were only used for

The Great Kitchen with some of Hardwick's collection of copper and brass utensils

storage, but the plasterwork overmantels and hooks for tapestry in the east and west turrets show that they were intended to be good bedchambers. The south turret, with Bess's arms over the door, a moulded ceiling and no fireplace was described in the building accounts as a banqueting room. The Elizabethan meaning of banquet was different from what it is today; it was a dessert course of sweetmeats, fruit and wine served either as a meal in itself or as a continuation of dinner or supper; like coffee today it tended to be served in a different room. Banqueting rooms and banqueting houses were often built where there was a good view; at Longleat in the 1560s Robert Smythson had con-

structed a whole series of banqueting rooms in turrets up on the roof, as at Hardwick. In general, flat roofs in Tudor houses tended to be used for exercise in good weather and for the enjoyment of the view; it was while walking on the leads of his house at Chelsea that Sir Thomas More was assaulted by a lunatic who attempted to throw him over the parapet. At Hardwick there were originally four banqueting rooms, the one in the turret on the roof, a second on the ground floor at the southern end of the east colonnade (now a bathroom with a mezzanine bedroom above it), a third in the garden house at the south-east corner of the garden, and a fourth in the north orchard, now the car-park.

Life at Harwick would, by modern standards, have been magnificent rather than comfortable. The food must always have arrived tepid in the High Great Chamber at the end of its long ceremonial route from the kitchen, and the guests, though they wore more clothes than we do today, must frequently have been even colder than the food. The huge multi-windowed rooms were only warmed by open fires; at the end of her life Bess was feeling the weather, as is shown by the coverlets and 'counterpoynt of tapestrie' described as hanging before the windows and doors of her bedchamber in the 1601 inventory. Lighting was entirely by candles. Water was pumped up by means of a horse-operated wheel from a well to a conduit house to the south of the hall. This survives, and originally contained a lead cistern under its canopy. From there a lead conduit conducted the water to the New Hall, perhaps to the two 'sesterns of lead' in the Low Larder in 1601. It must have been carried to other parts of the house in containers, for there was no form of running water system. Sanitation was equally crude; the Old Hall had a tower full of privies built out over the hillside, but this dates from after Bess's time; in the New Hall most bedrooms had chamber pots and close stools, the latter usually covered with leather. Bess had her personal close stool in a little room off her bedchamber; it was 'covered with blewe cloth sticht with white, with red and black silk fringe', but there were no backstairs and no amount of silk fringe can have offset the squalor of carrying the contents of the emptied close stools down the two great staircases.

Banqueting house and chimneys on the roof

CHAPTER FIVE

HARDWICK AFTER BESS

'Never was I less charmed in my life. The house is not Gothic, but of that betweenity, that intervened when Gothic declined and Palladian was creeping in – rather, this is totally naked of either . . . The gallery is sixty yards long, covered with bad tapestry and wretched pictures.'
Horace Walpole, 1760

'Some of the Appartments are large, but ill fitted up, & the general Disposition of the Rooms is awkward . . . I took notice of a good deal of old Stucco in the State Room representing Hastings, & the figures coloured, but it is very ugly.'
Philip Yorke, Lord Hardwicke, 1763

'Like a great old castle of romance . . . Such lofty magnificence! And built with stone, upon a hill! One of the proudest piles I ever beheld.'
John Byng, Lord Torrington, 1789

Bess was succeeded at Hardwick by her second son William, who had been created Baron Cavendish of Hardwick in 1605. When his elder brother Henry died in 1616 he inherited Chatsworth, but Hardwick remained his principal place of residence. In 1618 (in consideration of a payment of £10,000 to the Crown) he was created Earl of Devonshire.

Between 1608 and 1612 he spent £1163 5s 6d on Hardwick. The accounts were entered into a 'book of building' kept by John Ballechouse but unfortunately this has disappeared, and only the weekly totals survive, recorded in the general account book with no particulars. The sum is a considerable one in terms of Jacobean money values, and it remains mysterious what it was spent on. There is no individual building of any importance at Hardwick which can be assigned to this time, but it is possible that the panelling in the High Great Chamber and the moulded ceilings in the Hall, Long Gallery, Mary Queen of Scots Room and Banqueting Turret

date from it. There was a second spurt of building in 1619–21, when a new wing was put up at the east end of the Old Hall, but this has since disappeared.

In August 1619 the future Charles I, then Prince of Wales, came over from Welbeck, where he was staying with the Earl of Devonshire's cousin, the Earl of Newcastle, and dined at Hardwick. The payments made on the occasion are recorded in the Earl's account book. Presents were made to the servants of various neighbours, who came with gifts of food, including fish and fowl, cheeses, a calf, apples and apricots, and half a stag. Wages to fifteen cooks came to £15 5s 8d, and in addition 'John Burtram the London Cook' was paid £12 for himself, his workmen and a boy. £5 10s 0d was given 'to my Lady to play with the Prince at Cardes'. About £50 was handed out to 'the Prince's servants'. A sum of £3 6s 0d was given to 'the Musicians that came from court'; another payment of £0 5s 0d for 'playing at my Lady's Chamber window', suggests an agreeable picture of them performing on the colonnade roof outside what had been Bess's Withdrawing Chamber, while Lady Devonshire and the Prince played cards within.

The Earl of Devonshire died in 1626. His son the 2nd Earl only survived him by two years and died in 1628, aged 38. He was as extravagant as his father had been careful and in his short life managed to make a sizeable hole in the Devonshire estates. He married Christian Bruce, daughter of Lord Bruce of Kinloss, who gained something of a reputation as a wise and witty lady, survived her husband for many years, and nursed the properties back to financial solvency. Their years as Earl and Countess produced two mementoes which were to have a curious and eventful history at Hardwick, in the form of two canopies which were set up in the High Great Chamber and Long Gallery respectively. Canopies had originally been the prerogative of the royal

The 2nd Earl of Devonshire (2) and his wife, Christian Bruce (Chatsworth). Although the 2nd Earl died two years after his father, he stamped his identity upon Hardwick by the expensive furnishing of the house

family or of ambassadors, but in the sixteenth century were widely adopted by peers of the rank of earl and above and set up over a state couch or chair of state, on which they would sit to eat or receive visitors. The subsequent history of the two canopies and their period of spurious glory when they were accepted as the royal canopies of Mary, Queen of Scots, is described on page 73.

But the 2nd Earl's main claim to fame is that Thomas Hobbes, the philosopher and author of *Behemoth* and the *Leviathan*, entered his service when they were both young men just down from Oxford. According to John Aubrey, although ostensibly the Earl's tutor Hobbes mainly 'rode a hunting and hawking with him and kept his privy purse . . . His lord, who was a waster, sent him up and down to borrow money, and to get gentlemen to be bound for him, being ashamed to speak himself.' None the less the two men seem to have been genuinely fond of each other. After the 2nd

Earl's premature death Hobbes became tutor to his son, the 3rd Earl, who remained his patron and protector for the rest of his life. At the end of his long career he retired to Chatsworth and Hardwick. At Hardwick he used to sing prick-song very badly in his bed at night and to walk up and down the hill 'till he was in a great sweat, and then give the servants some money to rub him'. He believed these activities would preserve his life, and indeed he survived till the age of ninety-one. When the family moved from Chatsworth to Hardwick during his last illness he was carried on a feather bed into a coach, and moved with them. He died at Hardwick in 1679 and is buried in its parish church at Ault Hucknall, beneath an inscription which places his long service under two Earls of Devonshire before the fact that he was 'well known at home and abroad through the fame of his learning'. He is said to haunt the path under the walls of the Old Hall.

Hardwick was regularly used as an alternative residence to Chatsworth right through the seventeenth century, and was adapted to new fashions in house-arrangement. Towards the end of the century opposite and matching apartments, consisting of withdrawing chamber, bedchamber and closet or cabinet on the formal French model then in mode, were formed to either side of the great hall on the first floor; one was probably for the Earl and the other for his wife. Closets or cabinets, highly finished little private rooms where favoured guests would be received for a tête-a-tête conversation, were a new feature of upper class life. Bess's withdrawing chamber and bedchamber were adapted for one suite with modish new joinery in the bedchamber; and the room through her bedchamber, possibly the closet which used to accommodate her close stool, was redecorated as a cabinet. The Low Great Chamber, Ship Bedchamber and Tobies Chamber were similarly adapted as a second apartment, with the Ship Bedchamber enlarged at the expense of the Low Great Chamber. On the top floor the Pearl (now Blue) Bedchamber was refitted in the same style.

These bedchambers and closets all have richly moulded doors, chimneypieces and overmantels of high quality; a similar door leading from the Low Great Chamber to the Ship Bedchamber was removed by the 6th Duke. Their redecoration may

have been the result of visits by the Duke's architects William Talman and John Sturges; ten guineas was expended on the former in January 1687 'for Diet, Wine and Ale at Chatsworth and Hardwick being 7 weekes'.

The main purpose of Talman's visit to Derbyshire was to inaugurate the rebuilding of the south front at Chatsworth. In the next twenty years the 4th Earl (Duke of Devonshire from 1694) gradually remodelled or rebuilt the whole of Elizabethan Chatsworth. Odd fittings from the old house were sent over to Hardwick: wainscot came in 1690 and a chimneypiece in 1691. It is possible that the wainscot may have included the inlaid panels now framed on the Chapel staircase, and the coat of arms and window in the Mary, Queen of Scots' Room; and that the chimneypiece may have been the 'Marriage of Tobias' chimneypiece now in the Blue Bedroom. Once Chatsworth was rebuilt, Hardwick must have seemed completely out of date by comparison. Until the end of the eighteenth century it was used less and less by the Cavendishes. Semi-deserted by the family and in gentle decay, it began to acquire a

Thomas Hobbes, tutor to the 2nd and 3rd Earls of Devonshire (81). He died at Hardwick in 1679

reputation as a curiosity, an untouched survival from the past. This reputation was greatly boosted on completely spurious grounds; Hardwick became a place of pilgrimage as the house where Mary, Queen of Scots, had been imprisoned.

As early as 1708 Bishop Kennet stated in his *Memoirs of the Family of Cavendish* that 'her chamber and rooms of state, with her arms and other ensigns, are still remaining at Hardwick; her bed was taken away for plunder in the civil wars . . . ; some of her own royal work is still preserved.' Later generations of visitors thrilled with unjustifiable excitement as they walked through the rooms which had, in fact,

been built, decorated and furnished well after her execution. By the mid eighteenth century Bishop Kennet had been improved on, and two beds reputed to have been slept in by Mary were on show. In 1760 Horace Walpole reported that 'the great apartment is exactly what it was when the Queen of Scots was kept there'. In 1762, according to the poet Gray, 'one would think Mary, Queen of Scots, was but just walk'd down into the Park with her Guard for half an hour. Her Gallery, her room of audience, her antichamber, with the very canopies, chair of state, footstool, Lit-de-repos, Oratory, carpets, and hangings, just as she left them, a little tatter'd indeed, but the more venerable; and all preserved with religious care, and papered up in winter'. In 1794 Mrs Radcliffe, the author of the *Mysteries of Udolpho*, 'followed, not without emotion, the walk, which Mary had so often trodden, to the folding doors of the great hall' and described how on the top floor 'nearly all the apartments of it were allotted to Mary; some of them for state purposes; and the furniture is known by other proofs, than its appearance, to remain as she left it'.

One can see how all this came about. At Chatsworth the apartments where Mary actually had been imprisoned survived unaltered until their remodelling in the late seventeenth century. There was then nothing left at Chatsworth to connect it with Mary except for two buildings in the park. But interest in her, on the increase through the eighteenth century, naturally transferred itself to Hardwick, where there was a complete Elizabethan setting ready to receive it. No-one looked at the account books in the muniment room which would have shown up the whole story; and the top floor

(*Left and right*) Hardwick has become linked with Mary Queen of Scots through romantic legend, although the house was not built until after her execution. Nevertheless, with the accession of her son, James, to the English throne, the Cavendishes felt that the connection with the Stuarts should be emphasised and her portrait (11) together with those of her parents, husband and son were hung in the Long Gallery. In the eighteenth century Hardwick became a place of pilgrimage for those interested in the tragic Queen, and panelling, including her coat of arms, was brought over from Chatsworth to the Mary Queen of Scots Room to strengthen the link

rooms, complete with canopies, were ideal for adoption as her state rooms, as long as the embarrassing evidence of the coats of arms and a few dates were ignored. A touch of authenticity was added by placing a carved panel of her arms, probably brought over from Chatsworth, in the room that became known as her bedchamber.

The legend of Mary, Queen of Scots', imprisonment at Hardwick is indefensible but it is worth pointing out that many of the Elizabethan furnishings and fittings at Hardwick today were originally at Chatsworth in Mary's time there. The famous embroidered hangings of heroines of antiquity, for instance, now framed in the Hall and on the Chapel landing, were shown to eighteenth-century visitors as the work of Mary; this they certainly were not,

but they were equally certainly made for Chatsworth in and around 1575. Other embroideries at Hardwick carrying dates in the 1570s, and probably many of the undated ones, must originally have been at Chatsworth. So must many of the portraits, and much of the furniture; the inventory of Chatsworth made in 1601 shows that it was relatively unfurnished, and it must have been partially stripped to furnish Hardwick. More Elizabethan fittings came later, such as the overmantel in the Withdrawing Chamber, and, possibly, Mary's own coat of arms, the Marriage of Tobias chimneypiece in the Blue Room, and the intarsia panels on the Chapel staircase. So if Mary were to visit Hardwick today she would find much that would be familiar to her.

The extent of the family's abandonment of Hardwick in the eighteenth century can be exaggerated. Notes made by the antiquary Richard Gough in 1760 show that the Cavendishes were still visiting and receiving there, and that the Duke of Cumberland had slept there in 1759. But little or nothing seems to have been done in the way of redecorating or restoring the house. This period of relative neglect ended in the late 1780s, when the 5th Duke and his wife, the beautiful Georgiana, began to pay regular visits. In 1789 Lord Torrington recorded that 'much repair has been done within some last years', that the house was full of workmen, and that the dining room (the Low Great Chamber) was being repaired; he complained that all the new work was of deal 'and only befitting a farm-house'. It was around this period, probably about 1800, that the lower half of the chapel was closed off and converted into a Steward's Room. According to his son, the 5th Duke used to dine in the Low Great Chamber 'as he supped at Brooks's, with his hat on, which his friends gave as the reason for his being so fond of Hardwick' while his wife spent there 'the happy part of a harassed life'.

But it was his son, the 6th Duke, better known as the Bachelor Duke, who really left a mark on Hardwick; his influence there is almost as pervasive, though not as obvious, as that of Bess herself. He inherited from his father in 1811, at the age of twenty-one, and died in 1858. Spoilt, lovable, lively, extravagant, and cut off from public life by his increasing deafness, he more than spent his immense income on building, buying and entertaining at his numerous houses. He largely rebuilt Lismore Castle in Ireland and Bolton Abbey in Yorkshire, and embellished and enormously enlarged Chatsworth. He described what he had done at Chatsworth and Hardwick in a delightful and discursive *Handbook* written for his sister Lady Granville and published in 1845.

At Hardwick attempts to live in the High Great Chamber and Long Gallery were abandoned. Of the former the Duke records that 'for one winter I dined with my friends in this room, which was more dignified than entertaining, and, in spite of all precautions, exceedingly cold'. Similarly he describes 'a vain attempt we made to pass some evenings in the Long Gallery; although surrounded by screens, and sheltered by red baize curtains, the cold frosty East wind got the better of us'. Instead he fitted up the withdrawing room as a library (the bookcases have since been removed) and used the

The 6th Duke of Devonshire, surrounded by his Burlington relatives; lithograph by Charles Baugniet, 1852

Nineteenth-century watercolours of Hardwick painted for the 6th Duke. (*Above*) The Withdrawing Room by William Hunt; (*Below*) The Long Gallery by David Cox, showing Henry VIII and Henry VII from Holbein's mural at Whitehall, and the equestrian portrait of the Earl of Arundel; both now gone from Hardwick dining room, and Bess's drawing room and bed-room on the first floor; it was in Bess's bedroom that he died in his sleep in 1858.

But his activities extended over the whole house. Hardwick was very empty when he inherited it but he filled it with additional furniture, portraits and tapestry brought from his other houses, from Chatsworth, Chiswick, Londesborough in York-shire, and Devonshire House in London. His approach was visual and romantic rather than scholarly or historical. The water-colours painted for him by David Cox and other artists give an idea of what he was after – an effect of great, but mellow richness, and romantic light and shade. He was prepared to use anything old, including work of the sixteenth, seventeenth and eighteenth centuries, to contribute to this effect, and his extensions and alterations at his other houses, and the sale of Londesborough in 1845, provided him with a constant supply of redundant furnishings. The feeling Hardwick tends to give today, of being a house where tapestry is used almost like wallpaper, dates from his time; it used to be even stronger, for a good deal of tapestry has been removed at various times in this century. He was the first person to hang tapestries on the main staircase: 'the dreary white-wash of these walls wanted decoration'.

With a fine eye for silhouette and disregard for history he brought a late seventeeth-century state bed, wrongly called Mary's, from Chatsworth to the High Great Chamber and used the tester and back of another Chatsworth state bed of the same date to replace the canopy in the Long Gallery. The High Great Chamber canopy was restored for him by Crace, the London decorator, then found too 'glaring' for Hardwick, taken off to Chatsworth and replaced by a made-up one. He employed Crace endlessly to restore, remount, and sometimes copy embroidery or materials, which were then displayed framed, mounted on screens, or up-holstering Neo-Elizabethan stools and chairs; frames for the embroideries were made up out of the yards of seventeenth-century egg-and-dart moulding made available by the redecoration of the Scots Apartment at Chatsworth. He blocked up many windows in the Long Gallery 'making the room warmer and giving more space and a favour-

able light to the pictures'. He disinterred the Elizabethan 'Apollo and the Muses' overmantel from a packing-case at Chatsworth and set it up in the Withdrawing Chamber. He set up West-macott's statue of Mary, Queen of Scots, originally intended for Queen Mary's Bower at Chatsworth, in the Hall at Hardwick, though admitting that 'she represents popular belief and tradition in defiance of dates and facts'. What he did in the way of minor alterations and moving round doors and panelling will probably never be fully worked out. As he put it himself 'though it appears old and unaltered, there has been a great deal done in my time, to the house that "Bess of Hardwick" built'.

The Bachelor Duke was succeeded as 7th Duke by his cousin, William Cavendish, Earl of Burling-ton. He had married Blanche, the daughter of the 6th Duke's favourite sister Lady Carlisle, but she had died in 1840 and his daughter Lady Louisa Cavendish kept house for him. In 1865 she married Admiral Francis Egerton and left home, but in her later life her father and her brother, the 8th Duke, lent her Hardwick for the summer, up till her death in 1907. As a young woman, shortly after her father inherited, she regrettably destroyed the state bed in the High Great Chamber, on the grounds that it was 'entirely devoured by moth'. But for many years she was a loving and careful custodian, and she left a worthy memorial, in the form of the garden.

In the eighteenth century there had been no garden at all at Hardwick. In the 1830s Lady Louisa's mother, Lady Burlington, was lent the house by the 6th Duke and laid out a garden in the entrance court; she planted the cedars which are still there and elaborate flower beds, in the form of a huge E S, which were removed in this century. Lady Louisa herself laid out the main garden on the south of the house in about 1870. It occupies the site of the original Elizabethan garden, but the plan of its cross-shaped walks, between yew and hornbeam hedges, was entirely due to her.

Evelyn, Duchess of Devonshire, whose husband inherited as 9th Duke in 1908, describes how Lady Louisa 'used to sit in the morning in the gallery making sketches and notes – the sun streaming on to her white hair and widow's cap – and she loved to talk about what she hoped we should do when we in our turn should have the care of the place. I think she left a benign and kindly atmosphere'.

Lady Maud Baillie, eldest daughter of the 9th Duke and Duchess, was born in 1896 and died in 1974, nearly twenty years after Hardwick had passed to the Trust. Her recollections of her childhood spent in the house have proved invaluable for recalling its atmosphere at the turn of the century:

When we were children the house at Hardwick, large as it is, was kept quite beautifully during most of the year by only two housemaids, the 'odd' man and a daily lady (she was called a 'char' in those days), whose limited ambitions seemed to consist in a passion for scrubbing floors. As the whole ground floor is stone-flagged, the area involved was vast.

The housekeeper, an awe-inspiring little woman dressed in black silk, reigned supreme. She had a real love and a deep pride in the house. On one occasion, when asked if the house was haunted, she replied that once or twice Bess of Hardwick, who died some 350 years ago, had come to thank her for her care of the house, but, she added, 'Of course there are no ghosts'.

When the family went for their annual visit to Hardwick for shooting parties in the autumn, they were accompanied by an army of servants, every room was occupied, even some of the turrets, which were the footmen's bedrooms. The only access was across the roof, an alarming experience in the dark with a gale blowing. There was no gas or electricity, and the darkness of the rooms, lit only by a very small lamp or a candle, was terrifying.

By the time my family, consisting of my parents and seven children, first lived at Hardwick throughout the autumn and winter of 1908, four bathrooms had been installed. In Lady Louisa Egerton's day there were none. The hot water for the main bedroom and nursery floors had to be carried from one tap on the third floor landing. The portable baths used were of the 'hip' variety, or flat round ones, into which the hard worked maids poured a few inches of tepid water. Even with the addition of a nursery bathroom on the top floor, life was anything but luxurious. All the seven children lived up there with a nanny, under-nurse and nursery maid, also any visiting maids who might be staying at Hardwick with their 'ladies'. The older children had breakfast and tea on the refectory table in the Great Hall, supervised by the two governesses. (We had already had 40 minutes' lessons by then.) The 'school party' were promoted to the Dining Room for luncheon. If there were many visitors, we were relegated to our own table in the bay window, which had always been known as 'The Monkey House'. The 'nursery party' had all their meals upstairs in the Day Nursery, i.e. three nurses, the latest baby and any other child under five; after that age one was promoted to the Dining Room. The transportation of nursery meals was a major operation. The tray containing the food for 'meat meals' was carried by the 'Odd Man'. All the other meals were carried by the nursery maid, who was probably only 14 or 15, but had to put up her hair when she left home to go 'into service' and also wear dresses to her ankles. As there were 97 steps in all it can be appreciated that her life was a hard one (though, as I remember them, they were generally smiling and frequently singing).

We must have been remarkably fit as children, as we climbed up and down these steps many times a day. We had to be down in the schoolroom at 7.15 for three-quarters of an hour's work before breakfast at 8.0. We did over 6 hours of lessons a day, but only $3\frac{1}{2}$ on Saturdays, with a compulsory walk or ride morning or afternoon. Each activity meant a change of clothing, and the lacing up, or unlacing, of high laced boots. All clothing was under the supervision of the nanny, and was therefore kept on the nursery floor at the very top of the house. The idea of keeping coats downstairs or near the schoolroom was unheard of. There were two governesses, one French and one German, and not a word of English was allowed during meals. There was little co-operation between the two ladies, and, goaded by aggressive children, frequent Franco-Prussian wars took place.

During the Christmas holidays my brothers, sisters and any cousins who might be staying with us generally took part in a play. This was no voluntary or spontaneous effort which we enjoyed, quite the reverse. It entailed hours of work, both in learning our parts and in rehearsing. The first winter we spent at Hardwick, it was thought appropriate that we should act the Trial Scene from 'The Merchant of Venice', staged in the Long Gallery. It was a somewhat ambitious enterprise as the eldest actor (Portia) was only 14. I was the Duke, aged 12, and so deeply were the words drummed into me that I can quote the whole part now, at the age of 76.

In addition to the female staff, I think there were 6 men servants when we were at Hardwick. The butler; (the under-butler remained immured in his plateroom at Chatsworth); the groom of the chambers; the valet (my father's personal servant) and two footmen. All these travelled wherever the family moved. The 'Odd Man' was a permanent resident. One of his main tasks was the collection and distribution of oil lamps throughout the house. These had to be filled and cleaned daily. There were 14 on each tray, and they had to be placed in every room in use in the house. Another travelling retainer was Mr Green, the upholsterer. He prided himself that he had never brought any new materials for patching or lining, but had always 'used up some of the old'. This economy had a particularly disastrous effect on some of the tapestry, which was ruthlessly cut to fit the staircase walls. During the last few years of my mother's life at Hardwick, we reconstructed a large panel (complete with the exception of one border) of Verdure tapestry. It was in twenty-five different pieces, and the assembling was quite fascinating, a combined game of hunt-the-thimble and a jig-saw puzzle. I spent many hours on hands and knees tacking the 25 pieces together. My mother, who was a beautiful needlewoman, worked the joints till they were almost indistinguishable from the original weave. When all else failed, she painted in the missing pieces on beige repp of a rough texture, and one has to look very closely to distinguish the fake from the original.

The Duchess's own care of Hardwick lasted from 1908 until the National Trust took over the house in 1956. In her husband's lifetime the family only went there for a few weeks every year, but after his death in 1938 it was left to her as a dower house, and she lived there continuously except during the war. For fifty years her strong character, lively curiosity, and delicately incisive voice dominated the house. As Lady Maud explained, this period saw much careful restoration of the embroideries and tapestries at Hardwick. The Duchess repaired many of them herself, sitting with an assistant, often one of her daughters, in the window bay of the Low Great Chamber, where the light was best for restoration work. It was she who was responsible for reintroducing the rush matting (originally made locally) which is now such a feature of the house. After the Trust took over in 1956 she stayed as a tenant, but visited the house comparatively little in the years before her death in 1960.

Evelyn, Duchess of Devonshire, repairing a tapestry in the High Great Chamber. Portrait by Edward Halliday

CHAPTER SIX

THE HOUSE: EXTERIOR AND INTERIOR

THE APPROACH

The most dramatic approach to Hardwick is from the
south-west by the Hardwick Inn: the road climbs very
steeply up under the silhouette of the Old Hall, turns a
sharp bend past the great hole in the hillside which
marks the site of the quarry out of which the two
houses were built, passes the mainly sixteenth- and
seventeenth-century buildings of the stableyard on the
right and the gaunt ruins of the Old Hall on the left,
finally emerging in front of the gatehouse and cren-
ellated courtyard walls of the New Hall.

The Old Hall is now under the guardianship of the
Historic Buildings and Monuments Commission
(English Heritage). It is under repair and not at present
open to the public. Prominent in the long south front
which dominates the approach from the south-west
are the huge top-floor windows of its two great
chambers, the Hill Great Chamber by the hill and the
Forest Great Chamber by the road. Both retain

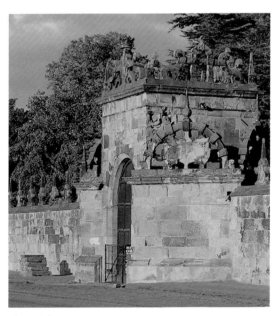

The gatehouse

considerable remains of their original plasterwork and
there are the remnants of fine plasterwork overmantels
scattered throughout the ruins.

THE FORECOURT

The gatehouse was also the porter's lodge and its two
tiny rooms were lived in until Victorian days; an old
lodge-keeper and his wife were the last people to
occupy it. In the centre of the balustrading above the
entrance is Bess's coat of arms and her supporters
carved in 1595 by Abraham Smith.

THE HALL

The Hall was used in Elizabethan days as both servants'
hall and entrance hall. The wooden tables and forms
relate to the former, the stone screen and fireplace
were intended to give dignity to the latter. The screen
was carved by William Griffin in 1597 and is a
remarkably pure piece of classical design for its date. It
supports a Gallery connecting the Drawing Room to
the Dining Room (Low Great Chamber); doors and
hatches originally gave access to the serving room and
buttery on the north side, and the pantry on the south.

Prominent over the chimneypiece is a plasterwork
overmantel of the Hardwick coat of arms, surmounted
by a countess's coronet and supported by two stags. A
stag with a collar of wild roses, or eglantines, was the
Hardwick family crest; three eglantines also form the
upper half of the Hardwick coat of arms, and the
flowers occur frequently in decoration and embroidery around the house. (The eglantine, a symbol
of chastity, was adopted by Queen Elizabeth as one of
her emblems and this may have provided Bess with an
added incentive for its use.) The Hardwick stags were
later adopted by the Cavendishes as supporters; coin-
cidentally their own coat of arms consisted of three
stags' heads. Painted on roundels in plasterwork
cartouches beneath the east windows of the Hall are
representations, perhaps early seventeenth century, of
the Cavendish crest, a knotted snake over the motto
'Cavendo tutus' ('Safe by being on guard').

PLANS OF THE HOUSE

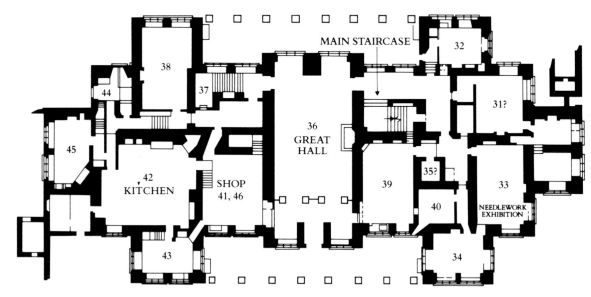

MAIN STAIRCASE

32

31?

38

44

37

45

36
GREAT
HALL

42
KITCHEN

SHOP
41, 46

39

35?

33

40

NEEDLEWORK
EXHIBITION

43

34

GROUND FLOOR

ROOMS OPEN TO THE PUBLIC ARE NAMED ON THE PLAN

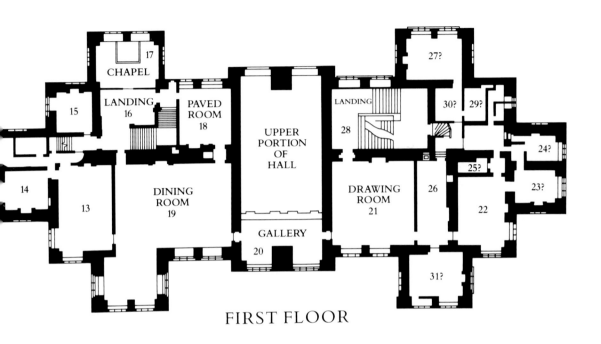

17

CHAPEL

LANDING
16

PAVED
ROOM
18

UPPER
PORTION
OF
HALL

LANDING
28

27?

30? 29?

15

14

13

DINING
ROOM
19

DRAWING
ROOM
21

26

24?

25?

22

23?

GALLERY
20

31?

FIRST FLOOR

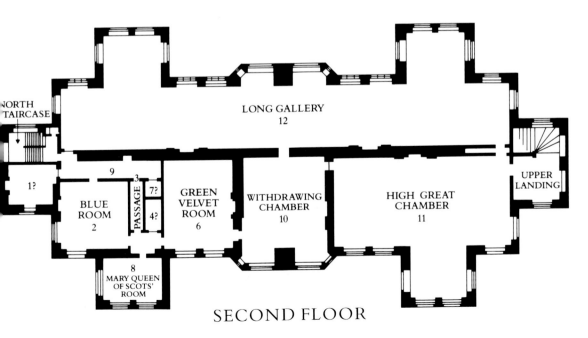

NORTH
STAIRCASE

LONG GALLERY
12

1?

9

3

7?

PASSAGE

4?

BLUE
ROOM
2

GREEN
VELVET
ROOM
6

WITHDRAWING
CHAMBER
10

HIGH GREAT
CHAMBER
11

UPPER
LANDING

8
MARY QUEEN
OF SCOTS'
ROOM

SECOND FLOOR

At the time of the 1601 inventory the furniture in the Hall consisted of three long tables, six forms, four wall sconces, two chandeliers and two firedogs. One Elizabethan table and two forms are still in the Hall but the massive oak central table, its top made of only two pieces of wood each $27\frac{1}{2}$ feet long, is mid seventeenth century. The seventeenth-century carved wooden chairs are all nineteenth-century introductions. Among them is the 'Revolution' chair, brought from the Cock and Pynot Inn at Whittington, near Chesterfield, and said to have been the chair in which the 4th Earl of Devonshire sat when plotting to bring William of Orange over as King of England in 1688. The great iron-bound wooden chest by the entrance is similar to one at the bottom of the main staircase, and these may well be the iron chests (probably money chests) listed in the 1601 inventory as in Bess's Withdrawing Chamber and Bedchamber. The armour is a miscellaneous selection mainly of the seventeenth century, brought down from one of the turrets in the nineteenth century. Between the windows at the east end of the Hall are the accoutrements of Lord John Cavendish, brother of the 9th Duke, who was killed in the First World War.

Note: ★ at the end of a picture description denotes a probable identification with a painting in the 1601 inventories. † denotes a definite identification.

The 1601 inventories were published in *The Journal of the Furniture History Society*, vol. VII, 1971; edited by Lindsay Boynton and Peter Thornton.

PICTURES

120 *Bess of Hardwick, Countess of Shrewsbury* (1527–1608)

Married (1) Robert Barlow, *c.*1543, (2) Sir William Cavendish, 1547, (3) Sir William St Loe, 1559 and (4) George Talbot, 6th Earl of Shrewsbury, 1567. For other portraits see Nos. 9 and 73, Gallery.

English School, *c.*1580, or a copy by Lockey. Apparently the pendant of the portrait of her last husband (No. 5, Gallery).

121 *William Cavendish, 2nd Earl of Devonshire* (1590–1628)

Succeeded his father in March 1626; married in 1608 Christian, daughter of Lord Bruce; father of the 3rd Earl (No. 24) and the Royalist hero, Charles Cavendish (Nos. 56 & 58). For other portraits see Nos. 2 and 57, Gallery.

Daniel Mytens, between 1626 and 1628.

EMBROIDERIES

The wooden screens at the end of the Hall were inserted early this century to contain pieces from two sets of hangings originally made for Chatsworth in the 1570s. They are made out of a patchwork of pieces of velvet, cloth of gold and figured silk, partly cut out of medieval copes. They are the most important Elizabethan embroideries in the house, and among the most important in existence. On the side facing the main body of the Hall are two hangings showing famous and worthy heroines between figures personifying their virtues – a theme that must have been congenial to Bess. To the left is Penelope with Perseverance and Patience, to the right Lucretia with Chastity and Liberality. These are part of a set of five originally in the Withdrawing Chamber. On the other side (in the Best Bedchamber in 1601) are panels of figures of virtues contrasted with historic characters who embodied their contrary vices. Faith

The plasterwork overmantel in the Entrance Hall, with the Hardwick family arms, two stags wearing collars of eglantine, supporting Bess's coat of arms and coronet as a countess

has her contrary, Mahomet, prostrate at her feet, and Temperance has the effeminate Sardanapalus in a similar position. Inset panels show Mahomet walking with his disciples and Sardanapalus feasting while his palace burns. Framed on the north wall opposite the fireplace are two panels embroidered in tent-stitch, showing the Judgement of Solomon and the Sacrifice of Isaac. In 1601 these were cushion covers in the Long Gallery. They are in the style of a professional workshop, probably French; several sets of embroidered valances in similar style are known. Solomon is watched by courtiers dressed in the style of the French court of Henri II. On the opposite wall are framed embroideries showing the story of the Prodigal Son, probably originally made for bed valances.

TAPESTRIES

In 1601 the Hall was hung with tapestries of 'personages with forestwork', possibly the fifteenth-century Hunting Tapestries now in the Victoria and Albert Museum. The present hangings were brought from Chatsworth by the 6th Duke. They consist of a set of Scenes of Country Life, from the workshop of Jakob Geubels I, and Proverbs. Both sets are from cartoons by Jacob Jordaens.

The passages beyond the stairs lead to the Needlework Exhibition.

PICTURES

195 *Landscape with Moses Striking the Rock*
Nothing is known about the origins of this picture: an old label on the back there is merely inscribed, 'Mr Simonds 73'. It is painted on a softwood panel, which suggests that it was done in Italy, although the artist seems to have been Flemish.
Italo-Flemish School, sixteenth century.

183 *William Cavendish, 6th Duke of Devonshire* (1790–1858)
Probably painted shortly before he succeeded to the dukedom in 1811, since the dog's collar is inscribed with his courtesy title as heir: *Lord Hartin[gton]*.
English School, early nineteenth century.

THE MAIN STAIRCASE:
LOWER HALF

In 1601 there was little in the way of furniture or fittings on the stairs, except beds, forms, and tables on the landings, for waiting or sleeping servants; the beds were made 'to turn up like Chestes' in order to conceal them during the day. The stairs were lit by a 'great glass Lanthorne' but the present one is a modern copy of the original lantern on the Chapel landing.

TAPESTRIES

There were originally no tapestries hanging on the Staircase; those there today were introduced either in or since the 6th Duke's time, and several have been ruthlessly cut to fit the wall space.

Octagonal canvas-work panels showing plants and herbs derived from sixteenth-century botanical plate books

Hero discovering Leander's drowned body from a set of tapestries telling the story of the doomed lovers, made at Mortlake in the seventeenth century

Along the first flight of steps is a set of tapestries brought by the 6th Duke from Chatsworth. Made at the factory founded by Charles I at Mortlake, Surrey, from a design by Francis Cleyn, they show the story of Hero and Leander. The scenes depicted include the first meeting of the two lovers, who lived on either side of the Hellespont; Leander swimming across on his nightly assignation with Hero; Hero's discovery of Leander's drowned body; and Hero's suicide. The set was designed in the 1620s and remained popular until well after 1660. The Hardwick set is one of the later examples and contains five of the seven known scenes in the series.

On busy days visitors leave the stairs and enter the Drawing Room from the passage that separated it from Bess's Bedchamber. Here are displayed, mounted in glazed screens by Evelyn, Duchess of Devonshire, early this century, thirty-two octagonal canvas-work panels reproducing designs from sixteenth-century botanical plate-books and bordered with mottos. Panels like these (many bear Bess's monogram) are also incorporated in the celebrated hangings now at Oxburgh Hall, Norfolk, which are known to have been worked on by Bess and Mary, Queen of Scots.

THE DRAWING ROOM PASSAGE

Five of these portraits (Nos. 141–145) are on loan from the Chatsworth Trust.

137 *The Hon. Richard Montagu* (1671–1697)
Second son of the 2nd Earl of Sandwich and Lady Anne Boyle (d.1671), fourth daughter of Richard Boyle, 2nd Earl of Cork and 1st Earl of Burlington (cf. No. 17).
Manner of Kneller.

145 *Lady Caroline Cavendish*, later *Countess of Bessborough* (1719–1760)
Eldest daughter of the 3rd Duke and wife of William, 2nd Earl of Bessborough.
Studio of George Knapton.

142 *Lady Betty Compton*, later *Countess of Burlington* (1760–1835)
Daughter of Charles, 7th Earl of Northampton, she brought Compton Place, Eastbourne, to the Dukes of Devonshire through her marriage to Lord George Cavendish (No. 176, Kitchen). Grandmother of the 7th Duke.
The Hon. Henry Richard Graves after Sir Joshua Reynolds.

141 *Lady Charlotte Boyle*, later *Marchioness of Hartington* (1731–1754)
Younger daughter of the 3rd Earl of Burlington and Lady Dorothy Savile, and sister of Dorothy (see Nos. 88 & 115). In 1748 she married William Cavendish, Marquess of Hartington, who became after her death, 4th Duke of Devonshire. It was through this marriage that Burlington House, Chiswick House, Londesborough (Lanesborough) and extensive estates in Ireland came to the Devonshire family.
George Knapton.

143 *Lady Georgiana Dorothy Cavendish*, later *Countess of Carlisle* (1783–1858)
Daughter of the 5th Duke of Devonshire, wife of George, 6th Earl of Carlisle. Engraved in 1790.
Thomas Hardy.

139 *? Lady Anne Cavendish, Lady Rich*
See No. 125, Lobby. Not previously identified, but resemblances to other portraits make it fairly likely that this is of Lady Rich. Bosom friend of Waller's 'Sacharissa' (see No. 140).
Manner of Van Dyck.

144 *William Cavendish, 4th Duke of Devonshire* (1720–64)
See No. 111, Dining Room.
Studio of George Knapton.

140 *Lady Penelope Spencer* (1642–1667)
Only daughter of Henry Spencer, 1st Earl of Sunderland, and Lady Dorothy Sydney, 'Sacharissa'.
After Lely.

138 *Lady Elizabeth Cecil, Countess of Devonshire*
See No. 23, Gallery.
After Van Dyck.

THE DRAWING ROOM
(1601 MY LADY'S WITHDRAWING CHAMBER)

The main door to the Drawing Room, off the Staircase landing, is surmounted by a splendid plasterwork cartouche framing a soldier's head under a flaming grenade. The head may have been intended to emphasise that servants armed with the 'three holberdes' mentioned in the inventory were on duty night and day on the landing to protect Bess's private rooms.

The room was used as a drawing room by Evelyn, Duchess of Devonshire, up till the end of her time at Hardwick, and has been left largely as she furnished it, with family photographs, Chinese pottery and mainly eighteenth-century furniture. The panelling probably comes from the Giant's Chamber in the Old Hall. The Elizabethan chimneypiece is decorated with the Hardwick stags supporting the arms of Hardwick impaling an incorrectly repainted quartering. In 1601 the furniture included a carved gilt and inlaid cupboard, an inlaid chest, a selection of other trunks and chests, a 'Chare of black lether guilded' complete with footstool, presumably for Bess, 'a little Chare of wrought cloth of gold' probably made for Arabella, and other chairs, stools and forms with cushions, including two 'chares for children'. On the wall hung a portrait of Bess and 'a glass with my Ladies Arms'; the latter still hangs in the room, a small verre-eglomisé panel of richly glowing colours, with the arms of Hardwick, and Talbot impaling Hardwick, surrounded by fruit and flowers.

TAPESTRIES

These are the 'six pieces of tapestrie hanginges with personages and my Ladies Armes in them' in the room in 1601. They are Flemish, possibly of Oudenarde manufacture, dating from the second half of the sixteenth century, and their subject has still not been identified. Like the Gideon tapestries in the Gallery they must have been bought from Sir William Hatton, as 'my Ladies Armes' were painted on pieces of cloth sewn over the Hatton arms; in all but one of the Drawing Room tapestries the Hardwick arms have been removed.

EMBROIDERIES

The framed panels showing Europa and the Bull, the Death of Actaeon, and the Fall of Phaeton are embroidered with Bess's initials and were all originally cushion covers; in 1601 they were in the Best Bedchamber, Gallery and Withdrawing Chamber.

FURNITURE

The early eighteenth-century Dutch marquetry cabinet houses a collection of blue-and-white china, prominent in which is a Ming porcelain jug with Elizabethan silver gilt mounts dated 1589. The four eighteenth-century chairs to either side of the cabinet have cross-stitch covers worked by Evelyn, Duchess of Devonshire.

PICTURES

82 *Sir William Paulet, 1st Marquess of Winchester* (? 1485–1572)
Created Earl of Winchester in 1550 and Marquess the following year. Godfather to the 1st Earl of Devonshire. He was Keeper of the Great Seal under Protector Somerset and a party to his overthrow.★
English School, sixteenth century.

83 *Lady Arabella Stuart* (1575–1615)
Daughter of Elizabeth Cavendish and Charles Stewart, Earl of Lennox, and granddaughter of Bess of Hard-

Ming porcelain jug with English silver-gilt mounts dated 1589

wick. Her position as claimant to the throne and her secret marriage with William Seymour, later 2nd Duke of Somerset, led to her imprisonment in 1611 in the Tower, where she subsequently died. This portrait of her was painted when she was two. For a portrait of her as an adolescent see No. 1 (Long Gallery).★
Unknown artist, 1577.

84 *King Edward VI* (1537–1553)
Derived from a full-length portrait at Hampton Court.★
After William Scrots.

85 *Henry Stewart, Lord Darnley* (1545–1567)
Son of Mathew Stewart, Earl of Lennox, and Lady Margaret Douglas. Married Mary, Queen of Scots, and created Duke of Albany, 1565. Murdered at Kirk-o'-Field. See also No. 126 (Lobby of Blue Room).★
English School, c.1561.

86 *King Henry VIII* (1491–1547)
Painted shortly before 1536, when the King 'caused his head to be polled and his beard to be knotted and no more shaven'.★
Unknown artist, c.1535.

87 (?) *Mary, Queen of Scots* (1542–1587)
When a prisoner of Queen Elizabeth, she was for fifteen years in the charge of the 6th Earl of Shrewsbury, but was never at Hardwick. For a certain portrait of this sitter, see No. 11 (Gallery).★
Unknown artist, sixteenth century.

MAIN STAIRCASE:
UPPER HALF

Prominent on the Drawing Room landing are two splendid late seventeenth-century tapestries, possibly of Brussels manufacture, showing two unidentified scenes from Roman history.

On the intermediate landing is a long table covered with a Turkish Star Ushak carpet, probably of the sixteenth century. This is one of three Turkish carpets at Hardwick which may be survivors of the thirty-two 'Turkey carpets' mentioned in the 1601 inventory. Most of these were used, as the Ushak is today, to cover tables or cupboards, but six were spread on the floor, including three laid around the bed in the Best Bedchamber.

On the landing outside the High Great Chamber, supported on a later wooden base, is a sixteenth-century table top inlaid with Bess's initials and a shield of Talbot and Hardwick arms. This may be

A panel of Hatton Garden tapestry, *c.*1680, showing boys at play

the 'inlayde borde' which in 1601 was in Bess's Withdrawing Chamber. It was probably set up on trestles when she wanted to eat in private. Bess's arms recur in plaster over the High Great Chamber door. The panelling of this is original, but it was reset and framed with later pilasters by the 6th Duke. The immensely elaborate late medieval lock was drawn by S. H. Grimm in 1785; it is probably German, and it remains uncertain whether it was on the door from the start or is a later addition.

TAPESTRIES

Running up from the Drawing Room landing are four panels of Hatton Garden tapestry showing children at play. One piece is marked HATTON GARDEN and signed with the initials of Francis Poyntz; the tapestries must date from between 1679 and 1685, when Poyntz and the Great Wardrobe, of which he was in charge, were in Hatton Garden. Opposite them, across the Staircase, a thin strip showing a portion of a lion hunt is all that survives of what must have been an early sixteenth-century Flemish tapestry of the highest quality; it would originally have formed part of a set depicting the story of Vasco de Gama or the Portuguese in India, which records show was very popular, and woven at Tournai. On the big intermediate landing are a selection of Flemish verdure tapestries of the mid sixteenth century; the one with a landscape along the top had been cut into strips and used to fill gaps in the Gallery. To the right of the entrance to the High Great Chamber, and above the Staircase, is a Flemish, probably Brussels, tapestry of the second half of the sixteenth century, showing sheep-shearing. Above the door is a Flemish Gothic panel of the first quarter of the sixteenth century showing, in strip cartoon fashion, David having his son Solomon crowned king, and Solomon, after his father's death, ordering the building of the Temple of Jerusalem. This and the lion hunt fragment are the earliest tapestries at Hardwick.

THE HIGH GREAT CHAMBER

This is the most undilutedly Elizabethan room in Hardwick, and the most magnificent. Its decoration was not completed until 1599, two years after Bess had moved into the house. The room was designed as a unity, with frieze, tapestry and chimneypiece fitted together into a whole glowing with incident and rich colour; the colours have faded, and the contrast between the sophistication of the tapestry and the crude but immensely evocative realism of the frieze is less strong than it must once have been. No records of payments survive for the relatively simple but very handsome chimneypiece, but it can reasonably be attributed to Thomas Accres. The ceiling is intentionally plain, as any plasterwork decoration would have obscured the frieze.

THE FRIEZE

Although not specifically documented in the accounts, this was almost certainly modelled by Abraham Smith and his assistants. Its theme is the forest, with the court of Diana prominent on the north side amid attendant deer, lions, elephants, camels, monkeys and other animals, and elsewhere scenes of deer and boar hunting, and of country life. To either side of the window recess, and rather more skilfully modelled than the rest of the frieze, are allegorical figures of Venus chastising Cupid and

Summer, based on Flemish engravings by Crispin van der Passe from designs by Martin de Vos. The frieze is interrupted over the fireplace by the royal arms supported by a lion and a dragon. The court of Diana, the virgin goddess and huntress, is probably a deliberate allusion to Elizabeth, the Virgin Queen. Bess must have had in mind a royal visit when commissioning these demonstrations of loyalty. The original paint survives on the frieze, much faded except for a small area in the south-east corner which has been clumsily restored and waxed. The frieze was almost certainly coloured by John Ballechouse, who was probably also responsible for the narrow strip of flat surface painting under the ceiling on the south and west sides.

TAPESTRIES

The tapestries were purchased in 1587, three years before the New Hall was begun, and the room must have been planned from the start to fit them. They are Brussels tapestries of the second half of the sixteenth century, from designs in the style of Michael Coxce. They have the Brussels mark and various weavers' marks, unidentifiable except for one mark of Nicholas Hellinck. They depict the story of Ulysses. In an anti-clockwise direction from the left of the Staircase door the panels show the following incidents (the numbers here show the chronological sequence, although to make them fit the space they were hung out of sequence):

Detail from the plasterwork frieze in the High Great Chamber showing Diana, the huntress, surrounded by her court. This is probably a deliberate allusion to Elizabeth I, the Virgin Queen, who Bess hoped would visit Hardwick

1. Ulysses kills a boar and is wounded in the leg.

2. His attempt to escape the Trojan expedition by feigning madness and yoking a horse and ox together is exposed when he swerves the team to avoid his infant son.

4. He identifies the young Achilles, whose mother has disguised him as a girl to save him from the Trojan expedition.

3. He departs for Troy and takes leave of his wife and her parents.

6. On his long and adventurous return from Troy he forces the enchantress Circe to restore his companions, whom she had turned into animals, to human form.

5. At Troy he is awarded the armour of Achilles who has been killed in battle.

7. He is shipwrecked, befriended by Princess Nausicaa, and given a new ship by her parents.

8. After twenty years he is reunited with Penelope and his son, having killed the suitors who were trying to force her to remarry.

PANELLING

In 1601 there were thirteen pictures in the room, including portraits of all but one of the Tudor monarchs. They probably hung in the window bay,

A detail of the top of the 'Eglantine Table' in the High Great Chamber elaborately inlaid with musical instruments, games and heraldic references to the Talbots and Cavendishes. It was made to celebrate the triple marriage contract between the two families in 1567: Bess to the Earl of Shrewsbury; Henry Cavendish to Grace Talbot; and Mary Cavendish to Gilbert Talbot. The engraving picks out clearly the details of the inlay

where the panelling now is. The panelling may have been introduced in the early seventeenth century in the time of the 1st Earl; the pilasters are additions, probably made by the 6th Duke. The panels are decorated with engravings consisting of a set of Roman emperors, and another of classical authors and philosophers.

FURNITURE

In 1601 Bess and her guests ate off a 'long table of white wood' covered with two carpets, probably alternatives, 'a fayre turkie Carpet' and a 'fayre long Carpet of silk nedlework with gold frenge, lyned with Crimson taffetie sarcenet'. When the table was

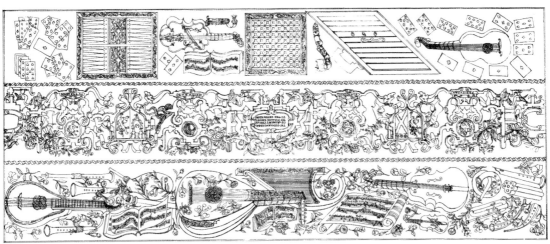

in use the carpets would have been covered or replaced by the diaper or damask tablecloths mentioned in the inventory. Bess sat in a 'chare of nedlework with gold and silk frenge' complete with footstool, and for the rest of the company there were six forms and sixteen stools, elaborately upholstered and cushioned. The only other furniture in the room was a looking glass (a rarity in Elizabethan days) decorated with the royal arms, an 'inlayde table in the window', a 'Cubberd guilt and carved with tills' and 'a payre of brass Andyrons' or firedogs, which can almost certainly be identified with the present magnificent brass ones, drawn in the room by Grimm in 1785. The 'Cubberd guilt' is probably the Du Cerceau cupboard, now in the Withdrawing Room. The 'inlayde table' may be the 'Eglantine Table' which stands in the window today, though this could also be the 'long table carved and inlayde' listed as in the Low Great Chamber in 1601. The eglantine table has certainly been in the High Great Chamber since the eighteenth century. It is elaborately inlaid with musical instruments, sheets of music (one has the motet 'Oh Lord in Thee is all my trust' set for four parts), cards, chess and backgammon boards, an inkhorn, the arms of Talbot impaling Hardwick and Cavendish impaling Talbot, and the Cavendish, Hardwick and Talbot crests and mottoes. In the centre two Hardwick stags support the motto:

The redolent smele of Aeglantyne
We stagges exault to the deveyne

The table may have been made to commemorate the triple marriage of Bess to the Earl of Shrewsbury, Henry Cavendish to Grace Talbot, and Mary Cavendish to Gilbert Talbot in 1567.

The existing chairs and stools are copies made in the 6th Duke's time (one is dated 1845) of originals probably of the seventeenth century. The originals were fitted up in 1635 when an entry in Christian, Countess of Devonshire's, account book records payment to 'George Savage the Imbroyderer' for seven weeks' work on the 'purple embroydered suite'. This embroidery was remounted for the 6th Duke on new brown velvet when the new chairs were made up; by then the original purple velvet had probably faded to brown. The 6th Duke also remounted in similar fashion the great embroidered canopy, bearing the arms of Countess Christian and her husband, the 2nd Earl, soon to be restored to the room. Another relic of Countess Christian in the High Great Chamber is her state couch, with sadly worn embroidery and her arms painted amid simulated embroidery on the wooden ends.

The two walnut mirrors hanging to either side of the window bay are late seventeenth-century English, as is the long-case clock, the works of which are dated 1697.

THE GALLERY

The 6th Duke described how people on a tour of the house 'begin to get weary and to think they have done, and to want their luncheon; but they are awakened when the tapestry over the door at the North end of this room is lifted up, and they find themselves in this stupendous and original apartment'. Measuring 162 feet long, 26 feet high and varying from 22 to 40 feet in width, the Hardwick Gallery is the largest (although not the longest) of surviving Elizabethan long galleries, and the only one to retain both its original tapestries and many of its original pictures. In 1601 it was sparsely furnished with two square inlaid tables, covered with carpets, three chairs, three low stools, a footstool, two forms, two mirrors, a little ivory table and a fire screen. In each window was a window seat furnished with a richly embroidered cushion. The embroideries often took the form of pictures; a number of these survive, and are framed in various parts of the house.

The frieze above the chimneypiece and tapestries was probably painted by John Ballechouse in 1598. If the two splendid chimneypieces, with their delicate and beautiful alabaster statues of Justice and Mercy, are by Thomas Accres, they are the culmination of his work at Hardwick. It is unlikely that the modelled plasterwork of the ceiling dates from Bess's time; it and similar ceilings at Hardwick may have been part of the undocumented alterations carried out by the 1st Earl after he inherited from Bess in 1608.

TAPESTRIES

The thirteen tapestries showing the story of Gideon and his triumph over the Midianites were bought by Bess when in London in 1592 from Sir William Newport (later Hatton), the nephew and heir of Sir Christopher Hatton, Elizabeth's favourite and Lord Chancellor. Hatton had died in 1591 leaving an estate heavily encumbered with debts, and Bess bought at least three sets of tapestry from his heir: the Gideon set, the Abraham set now in the Green Velvet Room, and the 'personages' in the Drawing Room. The cost of the Gideon set was £326 6s from which £5 was deducted because Bess had to change the Hatton arms to her own. In fact all that was done was to cover the Hatton shields with pieces of cloth painted with Bess's arms, and to add painted horns and collars to the Hatton does to convert them into Hardwick stags.

The tapestries had been made for Hatton in 1578 and probably originally hung at Holdenby, Northamptonshire, his principal house. They are 19 feet high, which is unusually large for tapestries, and are Flemish, probably made at Oudenarde. The colours have faded and the story is almost impossible to make out because of the pictures that cover the tapestries. At first they were probably unencumbered by pictures, but in the time of the 5th Duke the tapestries and all available wall space were covered with pictures of all dates, often hanging three deep.

FURNITURE

A drawing made in the Gallery by S. H. Grimm in 1785 shows Countess Christian's state couch (now in the High Great Chamber) beneath a plain canopy. The 6th Duke replaced this by a much more splendid canopy made out of the tester and head of the bed from the state bedroom at Chatsworth supplied by Francis Lapierre in 1697 and one of the most magnificent examples of late seventeenth-century upholstery surviving in England. It was installed at Hardwick as a piece of romantic stage scenery, for by the 6th Duke's time canopies had no functional purpose in a private house. Under it now are two high-backed chairs of carved walnut. With original red velvet upholstery appliquéd with silver thread, part of a set made about 1700 for the Queen of Scots' apartment at Chatsworth; five stools from the same suite are also in the Gallery. The whole set was brought over to Hardwick by the 6th Duke, and originally placed in the High Great Chamber along with the Scots' apartment bed. Three of the richly carved feet from this demolished late seventeenth-century bed are displayed on the window ledge. Along the opposite wall is a set of late seventeenth-century armed walnut chairs with high rectangular backs, and a set of circular and rectangular walnut stools of the same period; the circular stools have cushions with the remains of Elizabethan embroidery.

Two long tables in the room are covered by carpets in the Elizabethan manner. The great carpet of faded red and green silk enriched with gold and silver is a Persian sixteenth-century carpet of the kind that excited the wonder and admiration of European travellers who visited the court of Shah Abbas at Isfahan. Although it was probably woven within a decade or two of the building of the house, it has been at Hardwick less than a hundred years. The second

A brass chandelier, c.1600, probably German or Flemish

carpet is a blue ground Turkish medallion Ushak carpet and is one of the three Turkish carpets at Hardwick that may be survivors of the thirty-two mentioned in the 1601 inventory.

The two brass chandeliers are probably German or Flemish of the late sixteenth or early seventeenth century. On the table in the north-east alcove is a plate of Hispano-Moresque lustre ware of the fifteenth century. On the inner wall is a selection of china vases and jars of the seventeenth and eighteenth centuries. The plaster bust at the south end of the Gallery is of Thomas Hobbes, and stands beneath his portrait.

THE PICTURE COLLECTION

The Long Gallery is not only the most breathtaking room in Hardwick, it is also perhaps the most striking example of such a gallery anywhere in Britain. It is surprising therefore to realise that its present appearance is largely the creation of the 5th and 6th Dukes in the early nineteenth century.

When Horace Walpole visited the house in 1760, with all his enthusiasm for survivals of the past, the best he could say of it was: 'Gallery 60 yards long, a small Couch with a Canopy, bad tapestry, and worse pictures, mentioned in her [Bess of Hardwick's] Will'. This indicates that the Long Gallery had survived up to this time as an example of the classic English type for a great house, hung with portraits of British monarchs and members of the family. What it never aspired to be was an historical gallery of great figures from the history, not just of the family, but of the nation and even of Europe. The models in England for this latter form of gallery were two sixteenth-century collections; one brought together by Robert Dudley, Earl of Leicester; the second by John, Lord Lumley. Rather over 200 portraits adorned Lumley's various houses, and 183 those of Leicester, whereas Bess's will mentions 20 portraits in the Old Hall and 69 in the New Hall, 37 of them in the Long Gallery. The Long Gallery was thus hung much more sparsely than we see it today, not over the tapestries, but probably on the window walls opposite. The portraits were mostly small, and more than half of them were of royalty. The major family icons were in the Low Great Chamber.

After Bess's death, her son William employed Rowland Lockey to paint over 30 pictures, the majority of them copies, for Hardwick, just as Lumley had done, using other painters, for his collection. Lockey (*fl.* 1592–1616), who began as an assistant to Nicholas Hilliard and had already worked for Bess, is best known for the two copies he made of Holbein's great lost portrait of *Sir Thomas More and his family*; one is now in the National Portrait Gallery and the other is at Nostell Priory, Yorkshire. The copies he made for William Cavendish were likewise chiefly of family portraits – sometimes perhaps worked up from miniatures – but also included one of 'the Queene of Scotts' (of whom there was already a picture in his mother's collection – No. 11? – together with a double portrait of the Queen's parents, *James V and Mary of Guise*, No. 60, and another of *Mary and Darnley*, No. 126). The fact that Bess's husband, the Earl of Shrewsbury, had acted as the Scottish Queen's custodian gained especial significance for the Cavendish family after the succession of Mary's son James to the throne of England in 1603.

The 5th and 6th Dukes of Devonshire were not really inspired by collections like Leicester's or Lumley's when forming the great collection of portraits at Hardwick, they had simply benefited from the alliances of the Cavendishes over the centuries, bringing to the family whole collections as well as individual pictures of great men. The first massive influx took place under the 5th Duke, who is originally recorded in 1790 as repairing the tapestry – already hung with portraits – and intending to put everything back as it was. The 6th Duke set about selecting and weeding out from his various houses – from Chatsworth, Chiswick, Devonshire House, and from

Hardwick itself – the pictures that would complement his historicising redecoration of the room. Yet, since he was no antiquary, he was happy to hang them as some must already have been hung in the eighteenth century, in tiers of two, three or more pictures high; for as he himself said in his *Handbook*: 'The pictures, of little value separate, have become interesting as a series.'

The core of the older pictures was made up of royal portraits that had been hung here or in the other important rooms of the house by Bess of Hardwick. First and foremost was that of her own Sovereign (No. 35), the sole survivor of three portraits of *Elizabeth I* recorded in the house at Bess's death. *James I* is represented as a child (No. 22 – the portrait of him as King of England, No. 12, is a later introduction) and there is a partially surviving set of past monarchs (Nos. 74, 75 and 77–79). Then there are the portraits, or their replacements, of Bess's family and important relations: *Lady Arabella Stuart* (No. 1 – another is in the Drawing Room, No. 83); two of *Bess of Hardwick* herself (Nos. 9 and·73 – another is in the Entrance Hall, No. 120); just one each of two of her husbands, *Sir William Cavendish* (No. 7), and *George, 6th Earl of Shrewsbury* (No. 5); four of her children and their spouses: *William Cavendish, later 1st Earl of Devonshire* as a young man (No. 10), *Mary Cavendish, Countess of Shrewsbury* (No. 4), *Grace Talbot, Mrs Henry Cavendish* (No. 8), and *Charles Stewart, Earl of Lennox* (No. 26), husband of Elizabeth Cavendish; together with one of *Bishop Stephen Gardiner* (No. 61), godfather to Charles Cavendish; and various other historical figures, most of whom were probably there because of ties of patronage or political involvement.

The most conspicuous difference between the portraits recorded in the 1601 inventory and the early portraits hung by the 5th and 6th Dukes in the Long Gallery is, bizarrely, the addition of a number of fifteenth- and sixteenth-century Cavendishes: the first member of the family represented by a portrait in 1601 was *Thomas Cavendish* (No. 70?), the father of Bess's husband, Sir William. These were clearly not conjured out of thin air. Close examination of the purported portraits (still only in its early stages) reveals that a number of the portraits of historical figures that appear to have disappeared from the house since the 1601 inventory are, in fact, still there – but, having lost their real identities, are decked out with bogus inscriptions, coats of arms, and labels, to denote them as ancestors. (It would in fact have been almost unthinkable for anyone with the status of Sir William's forebears to have had themselves painted.) Thus, *Robert Dudley, Earl of Leicester* has become the dissolute *Henry*

Cavendish (No. 62). An extraordinarily rare portrait of *Protector Somerset* has been baptised as a fifteenth-century *Thomas Cavendish* (No. 64). The portrait of *Philip II of Spain* has been identified as another *Thomas Cavendish* (No. 67). The 'missing' portrait of the real *Thomas Cavendish* has been reidentified as Sir William's brother, *George Cavendish* (No. 70). A portrait of *Lord Keeper Bacon* has been turned into yet another of the legion of doubtful Thomases (No. 69).

It is clear from an inventory taken in 1792 that a number of seventeenth-century portraits had already been added to the Gallery. The additions made by the 5th and 6th Dukes did not pretend to be of the period of the room any more than these did, but went up as far as the *Lord Carleton* of 1703 (No. 31): anything of the seventeenth century – or just into the eighteenth – was evidently considered sufficiently historical to go there. The one 'sport' appears to be a portrait of *Queen Caroline and the Duke of Cumberland* (No. 30) from Chiswick House. The portraits installed were still primarily of dynastic interest, and even the historical figures were all aristocratic. The one exception was *Thomas Hobbes* (No. 81), who was included more in the guise of faithful family retainer, as tutor to the 2nd

and 3rd Earls and because he died in the house, rather than in that of a great philosopher.

It was as an extension of the old ideas of the Gallery as a repository of portraits of sovereigns that the 6th Duke also placed here representatives of foreign ruling families: *Louis XIV as a child* (No. 55); his brother, *Philippe, duc d'Orléans* as a young man (No. 42); the *Elector Palatine, Prince Charles Louis* (No. 47); and *Duke Christian of Brunswick-Wolfenbüttel* (No. 45). Bess of Hardwick had done the same, with portraits of *Henri III*, another *'French King'*, the *Emperor Charles V*, the *Duc de Bouillon*, and the *Duke of Alva*, but these have all disappeared.

A few additions and subtractions have been made to the pictures in the Gallery since the 6th Duke's day – chief among them being the removal of the surviving fragment, showing *Henry VIII*, of Holbein's cartoon for his mural in the palace of Whitehall (now in the National Portrait Gallery), and of the little, equestrian, posthumous portrait of *Henry, Earl of Arundel* (now at Chatsworth), both of which are conspicuous in the foreground of David Cox's view down the Long Gallery (p.43). Despite these losses, the hang of Hardwick's great Long Gallery is very much as – if a

The Long Gallery in the time of the 6th Duke, from a watercolour by David Cox

little thinner than – the 6th Duke left it, over a century ago.

1 *Lady Arabella Stuart* (1575–1615)
See No. 83 (Drawing Room).
(?) Rowland Lockey, after a portrait of 1589.

2 *William Cavendish, 2nd Earl of Devonshire* (1590–1628)
See No. 121, which shows the sitter only a year or two later, yet already much aged, and No. 57.
English School, 1625 or 1626.

3 (?) *Gilbert Talbot, 7th Earl of Shrewsbury* (1553–1616)
Married Mary, daughter of Sir William Cavendish and Bess of Hardwick, in 1567. The identification of the sitter as the 7th Earl is late and doubtful.
English School, 1590s.

4 *Mary Cavendish, Countess of Shrewsbury* (1555–1632)
Daughter of Sir William Cavendish and Bess of Hardwick and wife of the 7th Earl of Shrewsbury. (The inscription, *Queen Elizabeth*, is a later addition.)
English School, sixteenth century.★

5 *George Talbot, 6th Earl of Shrewsbury* (c.1528–1590)
Married Bess of Hardwick in 1567 as his second wife and her fourth husband. Acted as keeper to Mary, Queen of Scots, when held in custody, 1569–1584. Apparently the pendant of No. 120 (Entrance Hall).★
(?) Rowland Lockey after an original of 1580.

6 *Lady Diana Cecil, Countess of Elgin* (1596–1654)
Daughter of the 2nd Earl of Exeter; married first in 1624 Henry de Vere, Earl of Oxford (1593–1625), and secondly in 1629, Thomas Bruce, Earl of Elgin, whose sister married the 2nd Earl of Devonshire. The portcullis is dubiously said to symbolise the incarceration of her first husband prior to their marriage.
English School, ?1624–1625.

7 *Sir William Cavendish* (?1505–1557)
Married Bess of Hardwick in 1547 as his third wife and her second husband. Sir William, who was knighted in 1546, acted as agent for Henry VIII in the Dissolution of the Monasteries. No. 93 (Dining Room) is a copy of this.★
Attributed to John Bettes.
(On loan from the Chatsworth Trust.)

8 *Lady Grace Talbot, Mrs Henry Cavendish* (c.1562–after 1625)
Daughter of the 6th Earl of Shrewsbury. Married Henry, eldest son of Sir William Cavendish and Bess

of Hardwick, in 1567. The attribution is sometimes doubted, because she would not have been nineteen in 1591, as the inscription says. Like other mistakes in the inscription, this is the result of careless restoration. Her dress and the inscriptions denote her as defenceless before her reprobate husband, after the death of her father in 1590.
English School, 1591.

9 *Bess of Hardwick, Countess of Shrewsbury* (c.1527–1608)
See Nos. 73 and 120 (Entrance Hall). Shown as a widow and therefore probably painted between the death of her last husband in 1590, and 1601, when it may have been the picture listed in Lady Shrewsbury's Withdrawing Chamber.★
(?) Rowland Lockey.

10 *William Cavendish, 1st Earl of Devonshire* (1551–1626)
Second son of Sir William Cavendish and Bess of Hardwick; married (1) Anne Keighley and (2) Elizabeth Boughton; succeeded to Chatsworth, Hardwick and Oldcotes on the death of his elder brother; created Baron Cavendish, 1605, and Earl of Devonshire, 1618.
Unknown artist (Cornelis Ketel?), 1576.

11 *Mary, Queen of Scots* (1542–1587)
See No. 87 (Drawing Room). No. 11 is one of the best of the 'Sheffield' type of portrait (so-called from the belief that the original was painted when Mary was held prisoner there, although it was actually derived from a miniature). The table-covering bears what has been thought to be a signature, P. Oudry, and the date 1578. An embroiderer of this name was employed by the Queen of Scots from 1560 to 1567, but there seems no substance for the belief that he was the author of this portrait, and his name may have been added in the nineteenth century.
(?) Rowland Lockey.

12 *King James I* (1566–1625)
(Wrongly inscribed *Richard Boyle, Earl of Cork*.)
English School, early seventeenth century.

13 *Unidentified Portrait of a Lady (?Anne Keighley, Lady Cavendish)*
The inscription identifying the sitter as '*Mary Cavendish, Countess of Shrewsbury*' is the result of a confusion with No. 4. It is possibly a portrait of the 1st Earl's first wife painted when she was plain 'Mrs. Ann Cavendishe', of whom there was a picture in the Gallery in 1601.★
Attributed to Marc Gheeraerts.

14 *Lady Frances Cavendish, Lady Maynard*
(1593–1613)
Only daughter of 1st Earl of Devonshire and Anne
Keighley. Married *c.*1608 William Maynard, sub-
sequently Lord Maynard.
Style of Marc Gheeraerts.

15 *Matthew Stewart, 4th Earl of Lennox* (1516–1571)
Inscribed as Sir William St Loe, Bess's third husband,
but in fact the grandfather of James I and his cousin
Arabella Stuart.
English School, sixteenth century.★

16 *William Cecil, Lord Burghley* (1520–1598)
Lord High Treasurer and Chief Minister to Queen
Elizabeth.
After Marc Gheeraerts.

17 (?) *Col. Charles Cavendish* (1620–1643)
Probably the same sitter as in No. 56, but a little
older.
English School, *c.*1643.

18 *Philip Herbert, 4th Earl of Pembroke*
(1584–1650)
Made Lord Chamberlain to Charles I in 1626, but
abandoned him in the Civil War. Married first Lady
Susan Vere and secondly Lady Anne Clifford, the
Cumberland heiress and widow of the 3rd Earl of
Dorset. He was a patron of Van Dyck and of Inigo
Jones.
Daniel Mytens, 1634 (?).

19 *Robert Cecil, 1st Earl of Salisbury* (1563–1612)
Younger son of Lord Burghley. Created Earl of
Salisbury, 1605. Lord Privy Seal, 1597–1612. The
'little crook-backed Earl' only sat for his portrait
once, hence the proliferation of this likeness of him.
After John de Critz.

20 *Lucy Harington, Countess of Bedford* (d. 1627)
Daughter of the 1st Lord Harington of Exton.
Married the 3rd Earl of Bedford, 1594. She was a
friend and patron of Ben Jonson and took part in
several of his masques.
English School, 1620s.

21 *Robert Rich, 2nd Earl of Warwick* (1587–1658)
A Puritan who began by encouraging piracy against
Spain and the colonisation of America, and ended his
career as Lord High Admiral. His eldest son married
the 2nd Earl's daughter, Lady Anne Cavendish.
Daniel Mytens.

James I in a portrait painted when he was 8 (22)

22 *James I* (1566–1625) *as a child*
Brounckhorst's original (differently dressed) is in the
Scottish National Portrait Gallery. Brounckhorst was
subsequently forced to become Principal Painter to
the King in 1580, when he was caught illegally
attempting to export gold from Scotland that he had
mined in partnership with Nicholas Hilliard.★
(?) Rowland Lockey (after Arnold van Brounckhorst, 1574).

23 *Lady Elizabeth Cecil, Countess of Devonshire*
(1619–1689)
Second daughter of the 2nd Earl of Salisbury.
Married the 3rd Earl of Devonshire 1638/39. The
original of this picture is at Petworth House.
The inscription confuses her with the wife of the
2nd Earl.
After Van Dyck.

63

24 *William Cavendish, 3rd Earl of Devonshire*
(1617–1684)
Married Elizabeth Cecil, daughter of the 2nd Earl of
Salisbury. A Royalist, he was attainted by Parliament
and his estates sequestrated in 1642. The portrait does
not represent Lord Salisbury, despite the inscription.
Studio (?) of Lely.

25 *William Herbert, 3rd Earl of Pembroke* (1580–1630)
Married in 1604 Mary, daughter of the 7th Earl of
Shrewsbury and Mary Cavendish. Chancellor of
Oxford University, Lord Chamberlain, 1615–1626.
He and his brother the 4th Earl were Shakespeare's
'incomparable paire of brethren', to whom the First
Folio was dedicated in 1623.
Daniel Mytens.

26 (?) *Charles Stewart, later 5th Earl of Lennox* (1556–
1576) *as a child*
The sitter has also been identified as James V or James
VI of Scotland (James I of England), but his dress
rules out the first, and the lack of any resemblance to
the sitter in No. 22, the second.
Copy (?) of an original of *c.*1565.

27 *A Child (possibly Henry, Duke of Gloucester)*
Although this child looks regal and was tentatively
called Charles II in 1792, he wears no Order and
corresponds to no other picture of the future King.
English School, 1630s.

28 *Lady Elizabeth Montagu* (b. 1668/69)
Only daughter of the 2nd Earl of Sandwich (cf. No.
137) and Lady Anne or Lady Mary Boyle, daughter
of the 1st Earl of Burlington (No. 17). The later
inscription identifying her as the '1st Duchess of
Devonshire' (1640–1710) is ruled out by the sitter's
comparative youth.
Sir Godfrey Kneller, 1698.

29 *William Cavendish, 1st Duke of Devonshire*
(1640–1707)
Succeeded as 4th Earl of Devonshire in 1684 and
created Duke, 1694. Married Mary, daughter of
James, Duke of Ormonde. A supporter of William of
Orange, William appointed him Lord High Steward
at his coronation. For other portraits of the sitter, see
Nos. 102 (Dining Room), 118 (North Stairs).
Attributed to John Closterman.

30 *Queen Caroline* (1683–1737) *and the Duke of
Cumberland* (1721–1765)
The Queen Consort of George II with her third son,
William Augustus, created Duke of Cumberland in
1726. Acquired by Dorothy, Countess of Burlington,
as the Queen's Lady of the Bedchamber.
William Aikman.

31 *1st Lord Carleton* (d. 1725)
Henry Boyle, younger brother of the 2nd Earl of
Burlington, was created Lord Carleton in 1714. He
held a succession of ministerial posts, and from 1721
until his death was Lord President of the Council. He
left his London house, whose name is perpetuated by
Carlton House Terrace and Carlton Gardens, to the
Prince and Princess of Wales.
Sir Godfrey Kneller, 1703 (?).

32 *William Cavendish, 2nd Duke of Devonshire*
(1672–1729)
Married Rachel, daughter of Lord Russell, 1688.
Lord Steward of the Household, 1707–10 and 1714–
16. Lord President of the Council 1716–17.
Charles Jervas.

33 (?) *Heneage Montagu* (1670/71–1698)
Traditionally said to be Heneage, son of Robert
Montagu, 3rd Earl of Manchester, and Anne Yelver-
ton, whom he married in 1655.
English School, 1674.

34 Reputedly *Charles Boyle, 3rd Earl of Cork, 2nd Earl
of Burlington* (c.1662–1704)
Succeeded his grandfather as Earl in 1697/98, having

Queen Elizabeth I, possibly a portrait by Nicholas
Hilliard and his apprentice, Rowland Lockey, 1599 (35)

previously inherited the Barony of Clifford of Lanes-borough. Married Juliana, daughter of the Hon. Henry Noel in 1688. Father of the architect-Earl of Burlington.
Attributed to Sir Godfrey Kneller, 1695.

35 *Queen Elizabeth* (1533–1603)
The portrait concurs with others of the Armada type, painted after 1588, in which the Queen is character-ised by a rigid and hieratic expression and depicted almost as an impersonal image. The artist has in the past been associated with an R. Stevens, as well as with Gheeraerts. More recently, it has been suggested that this is the portrait of the Queen that was brought from London to Hardwick in 1599, and that it is from the workshop of Nicholas Hilliard. There are payments from Bess of Hardwick to Hilliard and his apprentice, Rowland Lockey, who specialised in oil paintings, for two 'picturs' in 1592.
(?) Nicholas Hilliard & Rowland Lockey, 1590s.

36 (?) *James Stanley, 7th Earl of Derby* (1607–1651)
The 'Martyr Earl', a Royalist who fought through-out the Civil War and was captured and executed after conducting Charles II to Boscobel.
After Van Dyck.

37 *Portrait of an Unknown Girl*
Formerly impossibly identified as 'Minette', Charles II's favourite sister, Henrietta, Duchess of Orleans.
Attributed to Robert Walker.
(On loan from the Chatsworth Trust.)

38 (?) *Richard, Earl of Arran* (1639–1685)
Although inscribed as 'James', (Scottish) Earl of Arran, much more probably his Irish namesake, the brother-in-law of the future 1st Duke of Devonshire.
Manner of William Wissing, 1684.

39 *Catherine of Braganza* (1638–1705)
Queen Consort of Charles II.
After Pieter Borsseler.

40 *Col. The Hon. John Russell* (1620–1681)
Variously identified in the past as the 4th Earl or the 1st Duke of Bedford, but neither is plausible. Though inscribed 'Lord Russell', this almost certainly shows the much portrayed Colonel Russell, the rival of the Comte de Grammont in the affections of 'la belle Hamilton' – Elizabeth Hamilton, ultimately Comtesse de Grammont (1641–1708).
Attributed to Johann Kerseboom.

41 *William Russell, 5th Earl and 1st Duke of Bedford* (1613–1700)
Grandfather of Rachel Russell, wife of the 2nd Duke of Devonshire.
Studio of Lely.

42 Possibly *Philippe, Duc d'Orléans* (1640–1701)
The identification with Monsieur, the brother of Louis XIV, is conjectural. Not painted from the life since the armour, which is datable to the 1660s, is incorrectly worn.
English School, (?) eighteenth century.

43 *Rachel Russell, Duchess of Devonshire* (1674–1725)
Daughter of 'The Patriot', William, Lord Russell, and wife of the 2nd Duke of Devonshire.
Sir Godfrey Kneller.

44 *An Unidentified Portrait of a Woman and Child*
Previously wrongly identified as Queen Anne and the Duke of Gloucester, who died in 1700.
Sir Godfrey Kneller, 1701.

45 *Christian, Duke of Brunswick-Wolfenbüttel* (1599–1626)
Known as the 'mad Halberstadter'. The most ener-getic protagonist of the Protestant cause and of the 'Winter Queen' in the Thirty Years' War, he died young and impoverished, worn out by successive defeats at the hands of the Catholic commander, Count Tilly. He wears the blue ribbon of the Order of the Garter, which he was accorded in 1624.
After Daniel Mytens.

46 *Unidentified Portrait of an Old Man*
Variously identified as the 3rd or the 4th Earl of Southampton, the sitter bears no resemblance to either. Natural beards and moustaches were unusual in England at this period, so it is possible that both sitter and artist were foreign. There is, however, some resemblance to Thomas Brudenell, 1st Earl of Cardigan (c.1582–1663) in J. M. Wright's portrait of 1658, now at Deene Park.
Unknown artist, c.1660.

47 *Prince Charles Louis* (1617–1680)
Elector Palatine, second son of Frederick V of Bohemia and elder brother of Prince Rupert of the Rhine. He made the first of a number of visits to England the year after this portrait was painted.
After Michiel Miereveld, 1634.

48 *Charles Boyle, 2nd Earl of Burlington* (c.1662–1704)
The discovery of an inscription apparently reading *C. Boyle* on the collar of the dog seems to indicate that this is a portrait of the same sitter as No. 34, before his acquisition of any title.
Sir Godfrey Kneller, c.1680–5.

49 Reputedly *Charles Cavendish* (1655–1670)
The traditional identification with the second son of the 3rd Earl of Devonshire is likely to be mistaken. The portrait derives from a drawing of the head of a sleeping youth in the Uffizi, ascribed to Manozzi.
After Vincenzo Manozzi.

50 *James Butler, 2nd Duke of Ormonde* (1665–1745)
Succeeded his grandfather in 1688. A supporter of William III and commander-in-chief of the army under Queen Anne, he was impeached at the Hanoverian succession and retired to France.
Attributed to Sir Godfrey Kneller.

51 (?) *3rd Earl of Devonshire* (1617–1684)
The inscription 'Gilbert Cavendish', referring to the 1st Earl's eldest son, who died young, can hardly apply to this later portrait. It has been associated with the 3rd Earl of Devonshire, and comparison with No. 24 makes it quite plausible that this could be him as a young man.
Manner of Cornelis Jonson, 1630s.

52 *John Churchill, 1st Duke of Marlborough* (1650–1722)
General and statesman.
After Kneller.

53 *Unidentified Portrait of a Man*
Style of Lely.

54 *Francis Clifford, 4th Earl of Cumberland* (1559–1641)
Son of Henry, 2nd Earl (1517–1570). Married Grisold Hughes, the widowed Lady Abergavenny, by whom he had Henry, 5th and last Earl (1592–1643), whose daughter Elizabeth married the 1st Earl of Burlington (No. 17), into whose family the barony of Clifford thus passed. The inscription 'Henry Clifford, Earl of Cumberland' is clearly impossible.
English School, early seventeenth century.

55 *Louis XIV* (1638–1715) *as a child*
Traditionally said to represent a Dauphin. It can be identified as the young Louis from the very similar, but superior, portrait in the Musée des Beaux-Arts, Orléans.
After Claude Deruet.

56 *Col. Charles Cavendish* (1620–1643)
Second son of the 2nd Earl of Devonshire. A Royalist general, killed while attempting to raise the siege of Gainsborough in Lincolnshire. For another portrait, see No. 58.
After Van Dyck.

57 *William Cavendish, 2nd Earl of Devonshire* (1590–1628)
Formerly wrongly inscribed *Gilbert, 7th Earl of*

James V of Scotland with Mary of Guise, the parents of Mary Queen of Scots (60)

Shrewsbury. Removal of this early nineteenth-century inscription has revealed traces of the Cavendish arms. By or after Daniel Mytens.

58 (?) *Charles Cavendish (c.1626–1659)*
Probably from Welbeck Abbey, since the informative inscription is typical of those put on under the direction of Lady Henrietta Cavendish Holles, Countess of Oxford, mother-in-law of the 2nd Duke of Portland (cf. No. 92).
English School, seventeenth century.

59 *Sir Francis Bacon, 1st Viscount St Albans* (1561–1626)
Lord Chancellor, 1618. Writer of philosophical, legal and literary works.
English School, early seventeenth century.

60 *James V of Scotland (1512–1542) and Mary of Guise* (1516–1560)
After the death of his first wife Madeleine de Valois, James married in 1538 Mary of Guise. She assumed the Regency in 1542 and was deposed in 1559. They were the parents of Mary, Queen of Scots. This is probably a native compilation from two separate French or Flemish originals.★
Unknown artist, sixteenth century.

61 *Stephen Gardiner (?1483–1555)*
Bishop of Winchester, 1531–50. Gained supreme political influence after the fall of Thomas Cromwell and inspired the Six Articles in 1539. Committed to the Tower by Edward VI in 1550. Godfather to Charles Cavendish.★
English School, sixteenth century.

62 *Robert Dudley, Earl of Leicester (?1532–1588)*
Formerly called Henry Cavendish, this is actually the portrait of 'The Erle of Leycester' recorded in the Withdrawing Chamber in 1601. Queen Elizabeth I's favourite, whom she long considered marrying. Suspected of murdering his first wife (the story adopted by Sir Walter Scott in *Kenilworth*), Amy Robsart, he repudiated his clandestine second marriage with Lady Sheffield to marry Lettice Knollys, Countess of Essex. Unsuccessful Governor of the United Provinces, 1586–88.★
Unknown artist, 1560s.

63 *Thomas Radcliffe, 3rd Earl of Sussex* (?1525–1583)
Lord Deputy of Ireland, 1556, and Lord President of the North, 1569. Assisted in negotiating Queen Mary's marriage with Philip II. Apparently already misidentified as Lord Treasurer Burghley when it was listed in the Low Great Chamber in 1601.★
English School, sixteenth century.

64 *Protector Somerset (?1506–1552)*
Impossibly inscribed with the name 'Thomas Cavendish' and the date '24th April 1453', this is in reality an extraordinarily rare thing, a genuine portrait of Protector Somerset, with the same likeness as that used by Nicholas Hilliard in his posthumous miniature of 1560 in the collection of the Duke of Buccleuch. Edward Seymour, 1st Earl of Hertford and 1st Duke of Somerset, was the brother of Henry VIII's third wife, Jane Seymour. He and Lord Paget manipulated the news of Henry's death to get Edward VI proclaimed king, with himself as Protector, in January 1547. He used his reign to push forward the Protestant revolution. Deposed in January 1550, beheaded for treason in January 1552.★
English School, sixteenth century.

65 *Catherine of Aragon (1485–1536)*
Daughter of Ferdinand and Isabella of Spain; married Henry VIII in 1509; divorced in 1533.
English School, sixteenth century.

66 *King Henry VIII (1491–1547)*
Not contemporary with the sitter.
Unknown artist.

67 *Philip II of Spain (1527–1598)*
Inscribed with the name of Thomas Cavendish some time in the nineteenth century.★
Unknown artist, sixteenth century.

68 *Cardinal Pole (1500–1558)*
Cardinal, 1536. His disapproval of Henry VIII's supremacy over the English Church made it impossible for him to return to England during the King's lifetime. Summoned to England by Mary and consecrated Archbishop of Canterbury, 1556.★
English School, sixteenth century.

69 *Sir Nicholas Bacon (1509–1579)*
Although inscribed and dated as though it were a portrait of Thomas Cavendish, Sir William's father, painted in 1515, this is actually a copy of a portrait at Corpus Christi College, Cambridge. Sir Nicholas was Lord Keeper of the Great Seal (1558–79), founder of his family's fortunes, and father of Francis (No. 59).★
English School, after an original of 1562.

70 *Supposed Portrait of George Cavendish* (1500–1561)
Brother of Sir William Cavendish, usher to Cardinal Wolsey and his biographer. There is, however, no portrait of George Cavendish listed in the 1601 inventory, in which the only portrait of an earlier Cavendish is of 'Mr. Thomas Cavendishe, father to Sir William Cavendishe' in the Low Great Chamber.

Since the purported portrait of Sir William's father is actually of Lord Keeper Bacon (No. 70), it seems very possible that this picture showing someone of around 1520, is a posthumous portrait of Thomas Cavendish. It was thought to be of Erasmus in 1792, before the coats of arms were added.★
English School, sixteenth century.

71 *Thomas, 2nd Lord Bruce of Kinloss, 1st Earl of Elgin* (1599–1663)
Second son of the 1st Baron (No. 72), created Earl in 1633. His sister Christian married the 2nd Earl of Devonshire.
Attributed to Daniel Mytens and studio.

72 *Edward Bruce, 1st Lord Kinloss and 1st Baron Bruce of Kinloss* (1548–1611)
Second son of Sir Edward Bruce of Blairhall, Edward Bruce prospered first as a lawyer and then as a judge, and was granted the Abbey of Kinloss in 1583. Thrice emissary from James VI to Elizabeth I about the succession to the throne, he was made Master of the Rolls when this took place in 1603, and Baron in 1608. Father to the 1st Earl of Elgin (No. 71).
English School, 1604.

73 (?) *Bess of Hardwick, Countess of Shrewsbury* (c.1527–1608)
See No. 120 (Entrance Hall). The portrait is inscribed 'Maria Regina', but is very probably of Bess of Hardwick, and the only portrait to show her in her prime and beauty, when she would have been married to Sir William Cavendish.
Follower of Hans Eworth.

74 *King Henry VIII* (1491–1547)
Derived from the portrait in Holbein's destroyed mural in the Palace of Whitehall.★
Unknown artist, after Holbein.

75 *King Henry VII* (1457–1509)
One of many copies of a lost original.★
Unknown artist.

76 *William Fitzwilliam, 1st Earl of Southampton* (1490–1542)
Raised to the peerage in 1537, Lord High Admiral, 1536–40. He married Mabel Clifford, sister of the 1st Earl of Cumberland. The portrait is wrongly inscribed 'Thomas More'.★
After Holbein.

77 *King Henry IV* (1367–1413)
One of many copies of a lost original.★
Unknown artist.

78 *King Henry VI* (1421–1471)
One of many copies of a lost original.★
Unknown artist.

79 *King Henry VII* (1457–1509)
A variant of the portrait type represented by No. 75.
Unknown artist.

80 *Henry Cary, 1st Viscount Falkland* (c.1575–1633)
Formerly in Burlington House, where it was unidentified. It is, however, of the 1st Viscount Falkland when Lord Deputy of Ireland (1622–1629).
English School, 1620s.

81 *Thomas Hobbes* (1588–1679)
The famous mathematician and political philosopher was tutor to the 2nd and 3rd Earls of Devonshire. According to John Aubrey 'there was a good painter at the Earl of Devonshire's in Derbyshire not long before Mr Hobbes dyed, who drew him with the great decayes of old age'. No. 81 is presumably the portrait referred to. He died at Hardwick.
English School, 1676.

THE WITHDRAWING CHAMBER

This room has gone through many vicissitudes. In Bess's time it rose as high as the High Great Chamber but some time before 1764 the upper portion was cut off to make a room on the mezzanine floor, where the original stone cornice mouldings can still be seen. By then it had become a bedroom. The 6th Duke converted it into a library, and it was the room in which he mainly lived when at Hardwick. In this century Evelyn, Duchess of Devonshire, took out the bookcases and made the room a state bedchamber. It has now been restored as a withdrawing chamber and the bed removed.

The alabaster overmantel carving of Apollo and the Nine Muses, with the royal arms and initials in the upper corners, was originally at Chatsworth, and was probably made for the high great chamber there in the 1570s. Eventually the 6th Duke brought it to Hardwick when he converted the room to a library.

TAPESTRIES

In 1601 the hangings of classical heroines and their accompanying virtues, which are now in the Hall and on the Chapel landing, were in this room, with the Abraham tapestries, now in the Green Velvet Room, as an alternative set. The present set of late sixteenth- or early seventeenth-century Flemish tapestries are thought to represent the story of Scipio or some other Roman general. The colours, unlike those in the Abraham tapestries next door, have

(*Right*) Alabaster overmantel of
Apollo and the Nine Muses
introduced to the Withdrawing
Chamber from Chatsworth in the
nineteenth century

(*Below*) Sea dog table of walnut,
one of the most important
surviving pieces of sixteenth-
century furniture

faded, so that the reds have turned brown and fawn and the greens a soft blue.

FURNITURE

The room now contains most of the comparatively few pieces of Elizabethan furniture surviving at Hardwick. Although some of these are identifiable in the inventory of 1601 their exact provenance remains so far undocumented; it is possible that the more sumptuous pieces came to Chatsworth in the 1570s and were either imported from abroad, or made by foreign craftsmen working in London.

Most notable are the walnut table supported by chimeras or sea dogs resting on tortoises, and the extravagantly pedimented walnut cupboard, both based on engraved designs of about 1560 by Du Cerceau, the sixteenth-century French architect. The

Walnut cupboard, decorated with pediments and based on a design c.1560 by Du Cerceau

sea dog table is perhaps the most important surviving piece of sixteenth-century furniture in England, of a regal quality which suggests it may originally have belonged to either Elizabeth or Mary and come to Bess as a gift. Similar beasts are shown on a state chair of Elizabeth's, as depicted in an engraving of 1575.

In 1601 the table ('a drawing table carved and guilt standing uppon sea doges inlayde with marble stones and wood') was in the Withdrawing Chamber; the cupboard was probably one of the two 'cupboards guilt and carved with tills' ('tills' are drawers or compartments) in the High Great Chamber and Withdrawing Chamber. A second, smaller cupboard decorated with Corinthian columns is also in the French manner but in the more classical style associated with Jean Goujon; it retains more gilding than the other two pieces. The two-tier cabinet with round-arched openings, also somewhat in the manner of Du Cerceau, might be somewhat inaccurately described as the 'cubberd guilt and inlayde with a marble stone in the side' in Arabella Stuart's chamber in 1601. The square games table inlaid with a board and playing cards is the only survivor of a number of inlaid tables listed in the 1601 inventory and is probably English work. The elaborate marquetry chest with arched panels in front inlaid with architectural scenes is in the German manner and has the initials GT inscribed on the keystones of the arches, probably standing for George or Gilbert Talbot.

PICTURE

129 *The Return of Ulysses to Penelope*
Bess of Hardwick's collection included a number of pictures that were not portraits: all but this and a vanished set of *The Four Continents* were religious in content. Bess clearly had a fondness for Penelope, who figures prominently in this picture, in the embroidered hanging now in the Hall, and in the Ulysses tapestries in the High Great Chamber. Presumably she identified herself with her, as a virtuous and faithful wife fond of spinning, or at least embroidery.

Correctly identified in the posthumous inventory of Bess's effects, by Horace Walpole's visit in 1760 the picture had acquired the fanciful designation of 'the Earl of Shrewsbury coming to court Elizabeth of Hardwicke'. A generation later, in 1790, it had lost all connection with Bess and was described to Arthur Young as showing Mary Queen of Scots in captivity working at her embroidery.★
English or Flemish, 1570.

The Return of Ulysses to Penelope, an English or Flemish
painting of 1570 that belonged to Bess (129)

THE GREEN VELVET ROOM
(1601 THE BEST BEDCHAMBER)

The elaborate surround to the door and chimneypiece is made of alabaster, blackstone and other
Derbyshire marbles and was put up in 1599 by
Thomas Accres, with the assistance of Henry Nayll
and Richard Mallory; the little figure of Charity over
the chimneypiece appears to be by the same sculptor
as the overmantel figures in the Gallery. In 1601 the
room was hung with seven embroidered hangings,
including the three embroideries of the Virtues and
their opposites, two of which are now in the Hall
and the remains of the third (Hope and Judas) in

store. It had an especially magnificent gilt bed with a
valance of cloth of gold and silver, and blue and red
curtains enriched with gold and silver trimmings.

TAPESTRIES

The late sixteenth-century Flemish tapestries were
the spare set of hangings for the Withdrawing
Chamber in 1601, and were bought in London in
July 1591 from Sir William Hatton and his agent.
Perhaps because they were not in regular use they are
still marvellously fresh in colour. They are a reduced
and simplified version of the famous Abraham set of
twelve pieces designed by Bernard Van Orley and
woven by William Pannemaker of Brussels about
1540. The subjects of the Hardwick set, starting to
the left of the chimneypiece and moving anti-clockwise, are Pharaoh returning Sarah to her husband
Abraham; Abraham being offered bread and wine
for his soldiers after the battle by the priest Melchi-

The Green Velvet Room with the eighteenth-century bed on the left and on the right the elaborate chimney-piece of Derbyshire marble made for Bess in 1599 by Thomas Accres

sadek; Eliezer, Abraham's servant, being offered water to drink by Rebecca; and Abraham entertaining the three angels who came to tell him of the destruction of Sodom and Gomorrah.

FURNITURE

The splendid early eighteenth-century green velvet bed with matching chairs was brought by the 6th Duke from Londesborough and must originally have been made for the 3rd Earl of Burlington, whose daughter brought Londesborough, Chiswick, Bolton Abbey, Lismore Castle and other Burlington properties into the Devonshire family. The richly carved and gilt stools dating from about 1685 were origin-

ally in the state bedchamber at Chatsworth and were brought over to Hardwick by the 6th Duke to accompany the tester of the Chatsworth state bed when he converted it into a canopy for the Gallery.

PICTURE

119 *Titian* (*c.*1485–1576) and *Andrea de' Franceschi* (d.1551)
Franceschi, Grand Chancellor of Venice, was a friend of Titian's, who portrayed him in the *Presentation of the Virgin* (now in the Accademia, Venice) and painted his portrait on several occasions.
After Titian.

MARY, QUEEN OF SCOTS' ROOM
(1601 THE LITTLE CHAMBER WITHIN THE BEST BEDCHAMBER)

This room is full of puzzles, but one of the few certain things about it is that Mary, Queen of Scots, was never in it. Over the door is a semi-circular panel enclosing the Scottish royal arms and the initials MR and bordered with the inscription 'Marie Stewart par la grace de dieu reyne d'Ecosse douariere de France'. The style of the coat of arms is very similar to that on Mary's own seal, now in the British Museum, and there is no reason to suppose that it does not date from her time. Its history has never been established, but it seems likely that it came from the Queen of Scots' apartment at Chatsworth, and was brought to Hardwick when Chatsworth was being rebuilt; it may have been among the 'wainscot' sent to Hardwick in 1690.

In general, the woodwork is much more elaborate than what was there at the time of the 1601 inventory, and seems to have been made up from a miscellany of sources. The door is dated 1599, and may be the original door made for the room. The little pedimented window looks at first sight to be seventeenth century, but although the glazing bars may be of this date the pediment is, in fact, very similar to that on the Du Cerceau cupboard now in the Withdrawing Chamber and may have originated from Elizabethan Chatsworth.

FURNITURE AND TAPESTRIES

The black velvet bed is a much restored version of one of the two beds which used to be shown as having belonged to Mary, Queen of Scots, and having been embroidered by her. There is no evidence and little likelihood of this. The bed may be a remake of the 'feild bedsted the postes being covered with black velvet' with hangings 'imbrodered with nedleworke flowers' which was in this room in 1601. The existing black velvet is nineteenth century, but is mounted with flowers and borders of Elizabethan embroidery.

The black lacquer furniture between the windows dates from the early eighteenth century; the four black lacquer chairs with matching day bed are exceptionally early examples of japanning, probably dating from the 1660s. The walls are hung with three pieces of Flemish verdure tapestry probably of the early seventeenth century.

THE BLUE ROOM
(1601 THE PEARL BEDCHAMBER)

The name in the 1601 inventory derived from the bed, long disappeared, which was embroidered with silver, gold and pearls, and probably dated from the time of the marriage of Bess and William Cavendish. The room is still hung with the four 'peeces of hanginges called the planetes' described in the 1601 inventory. These are Brussels tapestries of the second half of the sixteenth century, and in fact depict a mixed set of gods and planets; prominent on the wall between the window and the door to Mary, Queen of Scots' Room is Neptune in a sea chariot, with Venus up in the sky in a chariot drawn by doves.

The cornice and doors date from the late seventeenth century. The chimneypiece with its carved alabaster overmantel is probably the one brought to Hardwick from Chatsworth in 1691 at the time when Chatsworth was being remodelled; if so, it probably dates from the 1570s. The cipher in the middle panel is made up of the initials E.G. and M, presumably for Elizabeth and George Shrewsbury and Mary, Queen of Scots. A similar cipher is incorporated in the needlework hangings worked by Mary and Bess, now at Oxburgh Hall in Norfolk.

The subject of the overmantel is the marriage of Tobias to Sarah. According to the story as related in the Apocryphal Book of Tobit, Tobias set out with his dog from Nineveh to collect a debt in Media. On the way he aquired a magic fish and a servant, who was in fact an angel in disguise. In Media he stayed with a cousin, and discovered that his cousin's daughter Sarah was a great heiress but possessed by a devil who had so far destroyed seven husbands on their wedding nights. On advice from the angel that the heart and liver of the fish, if burnt, would produce a stench that would destroy the devil, Tobias married Sarah, with complete success. This story must have been a favourite of Bess's for she also owned a set of tapestries depicting it, and incidents from it decorate a big embroidered table carpet ornamented with her coat of arms (not on show at the moment) and dated 1579.

FURNITURE

The bed is based on one belonging to Christian Cavendish (née Bruce), wife of the 2nd Earl of Devonshire, and is embroidered with her arms and the date 1629, together with the arms of the 6th Duke and the date 1852. In the latter year the original embroidery was remounted on a new blue damask copying the original one. The eighteenth-century

The Blue Room, with Christian Bruce's bed of 1629 in the foreground and the marriage of Tobias to Sarah portrayed in the carved alabaster of the overmantel

mahogany chairs are covered with the same damask and mounted with seventeenth-century blue brocade en suite with that on the bed. The table veneered with walnut 'oyster marquetry' and the matching torchère (the survivor of a pair) is early eighteenth century, as are the other two torchères. The leather-covered chest studded with brass nails and royal crowns and bearing the date 1727 may be one of two 'strong boxes' which according to Lady Louisa Egerton were brought from Chiswick House in 1891.

THE LOBBY BETWEEN THE BLUE ROOM AND THE NORTH STAIRCASE

PANELLING

The panelling over the door to the stairs is decorated with engravings in the manner of that in the High Great Chamber and was removed by the 6th Duke from over a door in the Dining Room. The other piece of panelling, crudely painted with Hardwick and other arms, came from the Old Hall.

PICTURES

122 *Queen Mary II* (1662–1694)
After Kneller.

123 *King William III* (1650–1702)
After Kneller.

124 *Queen Anne* (1665–1714)
After Kneller.

125 *Lady Anne Cavendish, Lady Rich* (1612–1638)
Lady Anne Cavendish was the only daughter of the 2nd Earl of Devonshire. She married Robert, Lord Rich, eldest son of the 2nd Earl of Warwick, and ultimately 3rd Earl, in 1632. Her untimely death was celebrated in poems by Sidney Godolphin and Edmund Waller; the latter celebrating her passionate friendship with Lady Dorothy Sidney, his 'Sacharissa'.
After Van Dyck.

126 *Lord Darnley* (1545–1567) and *Mary Stuart* (1542–1587)
Darnley married Mary Stuart in 1565. The portrait is said to be unique in portraying the Queen of Scots during her reign in Scotland, but like No. 60, it is a composite image.★
Unknown artist, sixteenth century.

127 (?) *Col. Charles Cavendish* (1620–1643)
Probably an imaginary portrait of the son of the 2nd Earl of Devonshire (cf. Nos. 17, 56, Gallery). The figure is copied from a portrait by Mytens of Henry Rich, Earl of Holland, in the National Portrait Gallery; the head is an awkward substitution that corresponds to no known portrait.
After Daniel Mytens.

128 *John Manners, 1st Duke of Rutland* (1638–1711)
Created Marquess of Granby and Duke of Rutland, 1703. He was a supporter of William of Orange. It is possible that the mysterious, nocturnal urban scene in the background alludes to the escape of Princess Anne from Whitehall in the Glorious Revolution, following which she took refuge at Belvoir.
John Baptist Closterman.

A detail of the original seventeenth-century blue silk damask valance from Christian Bruce's bed next door

THE PASSAGE BY MARY, QUEEN OF SCOTS' ROOM

This is hung with a selection of framed embroideries of various dates including a panel of late medieval *opus anglicanum* work, probably made up from a cope orphrey, and one of the original valances of the Countess Christian bed in the Blue Room next door.

THE NORTH STAIRCASE

Each step is made of a single piece of oak and the stairs are lined with framed panels of embroidery, including some late medieval work, probably material from copes, and a set of symbolic figures of the Liberal Arts under arches.

THE DINING ROOM
(1601 THE LOW GREAT CHAMBER)

In 1601 this was richly and fully furnished for its various functions of sitting, eating and recreation, with a long table and cupboard for meals, two square tables for games and cards, pictures, curtains, eight tapestry hangings of the story of David and numerous richly trimmed and embroidered chairs, stools, forms and cushions. Everything Elizabethan has since disappeared except for the chimneypiece, dated 1597, with its rather clumsy plasterwork overmantel and inscription 'The conclusion of all thinges is to feare God and keepe his commaundementes', and the wall sconces, which may be the 'four plate Candlestickes of brass to hang on the wales' which were in the Hall in 1601; if so, one must be a later copy, for there are now five.

The room developed into a straightforward dining room and was slightly reduced in size in the late seventeenth century to enlarge the adjacent bedroom. It has been hung with eighteenth- and early nineteenth-century portraits since the time of the 6th Duke, who probably brought in the panelling from the Old Hall.

The deep window bay has served a number of uses. The 6th Duke as a boy 'turned the recess . . . into a kind of menagerie: a fishing net nailed up under the curtain confined the rabbits, hedgehogs, squirrels, guinea pigs, and white mice, that were the joy of his life from 8 to 12 years old, the smell caused by these quadrupeds was overpowering. . . . A tree stood in the middle for the unhappy birds – caught by John Hall the gamekeeper – to perch on, and an owl made its melancholy hooting in one of the corners.' In later life he installed a billiard table . . . 'connected in this manner with an inhabited room, nothing in the world – no nothing can be more enjoyable'. In the time of Evelyn, Duchess of Devonshire, the recess was much used for the repair of tapestries, as it has the best light for this purpose in the house.

FURNISHINGS

The furniture is mainly late eighteenth-century mahogany collected together from various places by Evelyn, Duchess of Devonshire, who thought the room 'a more effective setting for plate and pretty clothes than the over-decorated dining room at Chatsworth'. The mahogany sideboard is a later amalgamation of three late eighteenth-century pieces, a smaller sideboard and separate wine cooler and knife-container in the form of urns on pedestals. The three great brass dishes are probably seventeenth

century, of uncertain origin. The blue and white dinner service carrying the Devonshire arms is a recent importation from Chatsworth and is probably Staffordshire ware of the early nineteenth century; although very decorative it is not luxury ware and was probably originally made for use by the upper servants in the steward's room, or in the great dining room on public days.

PICTURES

88 *Lady Dorothy Boyle, Countess of Euston* (1724–1742)
Elder daughter of 3rd Earl of Burlington and Lady Dorothy Savile. Married in 1741 to George, Earl of Euston, heir to the 2nd Duke of Grafton.
George Knapton.

89 (?) *Lord James Cavendish* (after 1673–1751)
Previously identified as Lord Henry (1673–1700). The identification is doubtful, in view of an authentic

The Dining Room with its Elizabethan overmantel dated 1597. In the foreground is the deep window bay where the 6th Duke kept his menagerie

portrait of him in armour by Kneller elsewhere in the house (not on view). The third son of the 1st Duke of Devonshire, he married Elihu Yale's daughter, Anne.
Sir Godfrey Kneller, c.1715.

90 *Unidentified Portrait of a Man*
English School, early eighteenth century.

91 *Unidentified Portrait of a Man*
The pendant to No. 94. Both are probably by the same French artist working in England.
(?) French School, late seventeenth century.

92 *Unidentified Portrait of a Widow*
No. 92 was originally at Welbeck and the form of the inscription follows those of other pictures in that collection, which were put on sometimes, as in this case, inaccurately, under the direction of the Countess of Oxford around 1750 (cf. No. 58). In view of this provenance, it is most likely that this portrait is of one of the Ogle sisters, both of whom were widowed in 1617: Catherine (died 1629), wife of Sir Charles Cavendish of Welbeck, or Jane, wife of the 8th Earl of Shrewsbury.
Cornelis Jonson, c.1618.

93 *Sir William Cavendish* (?1505–1557)
See No. 7 (Gallery), of which this is a copy.
After John Bettes (?).

94 *Unidentified Portrait of a Man*
The pendant to No. 91.
(?) French School, late seventeenth century.

95 *Unidentified Portrait of a Young Man*
Before the discovery of the artist's signature and date this was thought to be of the 3rd Earl of Devonshire as a young man (cf. Nos. 24 and 51). If the date has been read correctly, this would be impossible, nor does the 3rd Earl appear to have had ginger hair.
Cornelis Jonson, 1631.

96 *Lady Dorothy Savile, Countess of Burlington* (1699–1758)
Daughter of William, Marquess of Halifax, married the 3rd Earl of Burlington in 1720. Lady of the Bedchamber to Queen Caroline. Mother-in-law of the 4th Duke of Devonshire. The artist was Kneller's assistant, and claimed to be his illegitimate son.
James Worsdale.

97 *Lady Elizabeth Cavendish, Wife of the Hon. John Ponsonby* (1723–1796)
Second daughter of the 3rd Duke of Devonshire; married in 1743 John Ponsonby, second son of the 1st Earl of Bessborough (No. 104). Whether or not they are in fact all by the same artist, this picture clearly forms a – possibly incomplete – set with Nos. 99, 100

and 104. They may have been painted for her family on the occasion of her marriage and going away.
Attributed to Jeremiah Davison, c.1743.

98 *Lady Dorothy Savile, Countess of Burlington* (1699–1758) *with her daughter, Lady Dorothy Boyle* (1724–1742)
For Lady Burlington, see No. 96, and for Lady Dorothy Boyle, see No. 116.
Michael Dahl.

99 *Lady Rachel Cavendish, Lady Walpole* (1727–1805)
Third daughter of the 3rd Duke of Devonshire. Married in 1748 Horatio Walpole, 2nd Baron Walpole of Wolterton. One of a set with Nos. 97, 100, and 104.
Attributed to Jeremiah Davison, c.1743.

100 *William Ponsonby, 2nd Earl of Bessborough* (1704–1793)
Married in 1739 Caroline, eldest daughter of the 3rd Duke of Devonshire. He was MP for various boroughs and Postmaster General, 1759–1762. In Turkish dress. One of a set with Nos. 97, 99 and 104.
Attributed to Jeremiah Davison, c.1743.

101 *Lord George Cavendish* (1728–1794)
Second son of the 3rd Duke of Devonshire, generally known as 'Truth and Daylight'. Inherited Holker from his cousin, Sir William Lowther.
Attributed to Mather Brown.

102 (?) *1st Duke of Devonshire* (1640–1707)
See Nos. 29 (Gallery) and 118 (North Stairs). The identity is uncertain, but this is conceivably a younger image of the 1st Duke as he is seen in the oval portrait set over the chimneypiece of the state drawing room at Chatsworth.
J. M. Wright.

103 *William Cavendish* (1783–1812)
Eldest son of Lord George Cavendish, 1st Earl of Burlington. He married Louisa, daughter of the 1st Lord Lismore, in 1807, and was the father of the 7th Duke of Devonshire. This picture appears to have been done as a preparation for Sanders's romantic full length of the sitter in fancy dress at Chatsworth.
George Sanders (after Hoppner).

104 *John Ponsonby* (1713–1787)
Second son of the 1st Earl of Bessborough. Married Elizabeth (No. 97), daughter of the 3rd Duke of Devonshire in 1743. Speaker of the Irish House of Commons, 1756–1771. In Hussar fancy dress, popularised by the dashing performance of Hungarian cavalry at the Battle of Dettingen in 1743. One of a set with Nos. 97, 99 and 100.
Attributed to Jeremiah Davison, c.1743.

105 Reputedly *Richard Montagu*
This is the title given to the picture by Lord Hawkesbury, but it is not clear who Richard Montagu was. It has been suggested that the sitter was a son of the 3rd Duke of Devonshire. Since it is similarly framed to Nos. 97, 99, 100 and 104, it is tempting to see it as a portrait of Horatio Walpole, added after his marriage to Lady Rachel Cavendish (No. 99) in 1748. English School, eighteenth century.

106 *Henry Greville* (1801–1872)
Brother of Charles Greville, the diarist; his own *Leaves From A Diary* was published after his death. John Jackson, RA.

107 *Lady Harriet Cavendish, Countess Granville* (1785–1862)
Second daughter of the 5th Duke of Devonshire. Married in 1809 Lord Granville Leveson-Gower, later Earl Granville. Thomas Barber.

108 *William Spencer Cavendish, 6th Duke of Devonshire* (1790–1858)
Responsible for the nineteenth-century additions to Chatsworth and the employment of Paxton in the gardens. See also No. 183 (School Room Passage). Somewhat puzzlingly, this is a pendant to the portrait of Lady Newburgh (No. 182). Orazio Manara.

109 *Lady Caroline Gordon, Lady Chesham* (d. 1866)
Daughter of the 9th Marquess of Huntly. Married in 1814 Charles Compton Cavendish, 1st Lord Chesham, fourth son of the 1st Earl of Burlington of the 2nd creation. Thomas Barber.

110 *William Lascelles* (1720–1764)
Third son of the 2nd Earl of Harewood. Married Lady Caroline Howard, daughter of the 6th Earl of Carlisle, niece of the 6th Duke. John Jackson, RA.

111 *William Cavendish, 4th Duke of Devonshire* (1720–1764)
In 1748 married Charlotte Boyle, Baroness Clifford, daughter of the 3rd Earl of Burlington, bringing the Barony of Clifford into the Cavendish family. He was Prime Minister, 1756–1757. See also No. 144 (Drawing Room Passage). After Thomas Hudson (?).

112 *Lady Dorothy Savile, Countess of Burlington* (1699–1758)
See No. 96. Manner of Kneller.

113 *Lord Henry Pelham* (1695–1754)
First Lord of the Treasury and Chancellor of the Exchequer, 1743. With his brother, the Duke of Newcastle, remained supreme in Parliament from 1746 until his death. A crony of Horatio Walpole (No. 114). After (?) John Shackleton, c.1752.

114 *Horatio Walpole, 1st Baron Walpole of Wolterton* (1678–1757)
Younger brother of Sir Robert Walpole, and father of Horatio Walpole, 2nd Baron Walpole of Wolterton, the husband of Rachel Cavendish (No. 99). It was because of his son's marriage that he solicited a peerage. MP for fifty-five years and a seasoned diplomat, he built Wolterton Hall, Norfolk. After Jean-Baptiste Van Loo.

115 *Lady Dorothy Boyle, Countess of Euston*, and *Lady Charlotte Boyle, Marchioness of Hartington*
See Nos. 88 and 141 (Drawing Room Passage). Reputedly painted by their mother (also portrayed in Nos. 96 and 112), by whom there is a signed portrait of Princess Amelia at Chatsworth. (?) Lady Dorothy Savile, Countess of Burlington.

116 *Lady Margaret Cavendish Harley, Duchess of Portland* (1715–1785)
Daughter and heiress of the 2nd Earl of Oxford. In 1734 married the 2nd Duke of Portland. Copied from a full length of her as a shepherdess, formerly at Welbeck Abbey, painted at about the age when she was celebrated by Matthew Prior as 'my noble, lovely little Peggy'. The label perpetuates an old error about the identity of the sitter. After Michael Dahl.

THE PAVED ROOM
(1601 THE LITTLE DINING CHAMBER)

As this room was originally intended to be the first floor landing of the Staircase, it has stone paving like the staircase landings elsewhere in the house, instead of being cemented for rush matting like the other rooms. In 1601 it was simply furnished and had no tapestries or hangings. The handsome overmantel plaster relief shows Ceres with a cornucopia. The date 1588 in the plasterwork is probably an ignorant repainting of the original date (1598) which had been defaced.

EMBROIDERIES
The room is now used to display a selection of some of the most interesting of the framed embroideries. Perhaps the most intriguing among these are the two

One of the sixteenth-century embroideries on display in the Paved Room. Detail of a cushion cover of velvet with applied pieces showing the 'Fancie of the Fowler' returning from the chase to his family

small panels to the right of the chimneypiece, each with five medallions copied in petit point from Faerno's *Book of Fables*. The centre scene on one panel, showing the frogs on the well-head, has the crowned monogram of Mary, Queen of Scots, and the medallions are set on an interlaced background of roses, thistles and lilies in allusion to Mary's double crown of France and Scotland and her claim to the throne of England. These are the only pieces of needlework at Hardwick which can positively be claimed as Mary's work.

A handsome table carpet showing the Judgement of Paris framed by the Hardwick stags and arms is dated 1574 and worked in the finest petit point, with over four hundred stitches to the square inch. Among a number of framed cushion covers is one showing a pear tree with its branches breaking under too heavy a crop, another of crimson silk worked in long-armed cross- or tent-stitches with numerous varieties of oak leaves, and two red velvet covers with couched silver-gilt thread and applied cloth of silver; the latter have been selected as examples of a style much favoured by Bess and her children. To the right of these is a cushion cover which in 1601 was in the Gallery and is probably based on a Flemish engraving from a set of the Four Seasons. It represents Winter, with a fowler returning from the chase as the central figure. To his left is a seated lady under a tree; a little shield of the Keighley arms between the initials AC has been attached to the tree to identify the lady as Anne Keighley, first wife of Bess's son William Cavendish, later 1st Earl of Devonshire, but this may be a later insertion.

FURNITURE

The folding wooden table is an interesting example of a type of table called a 'Spanish table' in seventeenth-century inventories: they were for occasional use, and were never meant to be displayed without a cloth.

THE CHAPEL

The lower chapel was shut off by the 5th Duke to make a steward's room for the upper servants; by 1800 these were no longer gentlemen and gentlewomen but they were still accustomed to live in some style and be waited on by the lower servants. The exact original size and arrangement of the upper chapel is uncertain. The present communion rails have been made up, probably in the nineteenth century, from a miscellany of original panelling. The pulpit was brought up from the lower chapel and is probably seventeenth century. The four wall hangings, painted with scenes from the Acts of the Apostles and with the Hardwick arms, are not identifiable in the 1601 inventory, but may be those for which John Ballechouse was paid in 1599–1600. Such painted cloths were a cheap alternative to tapestry, the style of which they imitated; they were common in the sixteenth century but the Hardwick ones are among only a very few that have survived.

PICTURE

196 *Madonna and Child*

Two pictures of 'Our Ladie the Virgin Marie' are recorded in the 1601 inventory, in the Gallery and the Low Great Chamber respectively, but it would be hazardous to identify either with this painting. Flemish (?), early sixteenth century.

The Chapel with its wooden screen

THE CHAPEL STAIRS AND LANDING

The two stone doorcases were carved in 1596, the one leading to the wooden stairs is by William Griffin and Adams and the other, to the chapel, is by Nayl and Mallory. Neither ever had more than one pilaster; there are no specific payments in the accounts for the splendid plasterwork cartouches enclosing heads, in the same style as that over the door to the Drawing Room.

The hanging lantern on the landing is probably the 'great glass Lanthorne' of the 1601 inventory. The big oak chest by the chapel screen conceals a hot plate for the Dining Room, installed by Evelyn, Duchess of Devonshire. The two embroidered hangings of Zenobia with Magnanimity and Prudence, and Artemisia with Piety (filial piety) and Constancy are part of the same series as the two in the Hall, and were originally in the Withdrawing Chamber. The Artemisia hanging is dated 1573; Piety is exemplified by the Athenian Pero breast-feeding her father through the bars of his prison cell. The four intarsia panels of stained and inlaid wood framed on the Staircase were brought over by the 6th Duke from the Old Hall; one of them is dated 1576 and there is little doubt that they were originally at Chatsworth, where many of the rooms in the Elizabethan house were lined with inlaid panelling. The Staircase panels are remarkable examples of direct Renaissance influence in Elizabethan England; they are probably based on engravings that have not been identified.

PICTURES

117 *Mrs. Knott* (?)
Said to have been a maid of honour to Catherine of Braganza, born a Stanley and married to a Mr Knott. But it is more probable that it simply shows the Virgin Annunciate, and that it was painted for Lady Mary Butler, wife of the 1st Duke of Devonshire, who had a private oratory in her apartment, and may even have been a crypto-Catholic.
William Wissing.

118 *1st Duke of Devonshire* (1640–1707)
See Nos. 29 (Gallery) and 102 (Dining Room). Originally painted for the clubroom of the Honourable Order of Little Bedlam at Burghley House. Each member of this precursor of the Kit-Cat Club had his portrait painted with his emblematic animal in it. The Duke's was a leopard, just visible bottom left.
Sir Godfrey Kneller.

THE KITCHEN

In Elizabethan times cooking was done at huge open fires in the kitchen, except for baking, which took place in brick-lined ovens in the pantry, a separate room in the north turret. In 1601 the kitchen equipment consisted of copper and brass pans, a brass kettle, a brass pestle and mortar, a frying pan, a chopping knife, a mincing knife, a cleaver, a gridiron, a grater, ten spits, five dripping pans, a skimmer and a hatchet. Open fires continued to be used until the nineteenth century, and over one of the fireplace arches is fixed a late eighteenth-century brass and iron bracket for supporting spits. In the late seventeenth century a crude precursor of the kitchen range, known as a stewing hearth, began to be used and there is a rare survivor of one of these, probably installed in the eighteenth century, under the kitchen window. It consists of a series of plates each of which was heated separately by charcoal placed in an arched recess without a flue. The stewing hearth gradually developed into the one-fire closed Victorian cast-iron range, and two of these were fitted into the original Elizabethan chimney opening. The robustly solid kitchen furniture was probably installed by the 6th Duke; the splendid collection of copper kitchen utensils, all engraved with the Devonshire crest or arms, date from the eighteenth and nineteenth centuries. The hatchment bears the arms of the 6th Duke, and was painted for his funeral in 1858.

A serving hatch connected the Kitchen with the original 'surveying' or serving room, which has long been joined with what was the pantry and is now the shop.

PICTURE

176 *Lord George Cavendish, 1st Earl of Burlington* (1754–1834)
Third son of the 4th Duke of Devonshire and Lady Charlotte Boyle, Baroness Clifford, heiress of the last Earl of Burlington and Cork, Lord George Cavendish had the earldom of Burlington revived in his favour in 1831.
According to the 6th Duke, painted by the sitter's cook; if so, perhaps copied from a Batoni.

CHAPTER SEVEN

THE ESTATE, PARK AND GARDEN

The name Hardwick means 'sheep farm', a clue to the hilly and wooded pastureland on which it is situated. However, to the south and west of the present house there is some evidence of ridge and furrow on the steep banks, accompanied by small settlements, which suggests that in places the land was ploughed. This probably took place in the thirteenth century when population increases meant that even unpromising land was brought into arable use.

Hardwick is not mentioned in the Domesday Book of 1087. Instead the parish of Ault Hucknall was divided into three manors, almost entirely in the hands of one Steinulf and forming part of a compact block of land with scattered settlements. Hardwick then was merely part of one of these manors, not a separate entity. The parish church of Hucknall, still isolated and surrounded by woods, contains Norman work and stood at the heart of Steinulf's estate. In the succeeding centuries, chapels

The towers of Bess's two houses at Hardwick as seen from across the valley

were founded in the surrounding villages, but they were subordinate to Hucknall church which remained the religious centre of the parish.

Stainsby, one of the component manors of Ault Hucknall parish, was held in the thirteenth century by the Savage family, who kept it until 1593, and the first mention of Bess's family comes with the marriage of her ancestor, Jocelyn de Haramere, to Isabella le Savage. Hardwick was probably granted to Jocelyn and Isabella early in the thirteenth century as part of their marriage jointure. Jocelyn called himself de Steynsby, while his descendants came to be known as de Hardwick.

By the end of the thirteenth century the de Steynsbys were an important and influential family, established at Hardwick. They were also benefactors of the Nottinghamshire abbey of Newstead, which had been founded by Henry II in about 1170, with the grant of Hucknall church. Where the Crown led, the local families followed, so that Jocelyn gave gifts of serfs and chattels, and grants of land to the abbey of Augustinian canons that, centuries later, was to become famous as the home of the poet, Lord Byron.

When Bess's grandfather, John Hardwick, died in 1507, he left an estate of four hundred acres in and around Hardwick. But the next years were to be hard ones for the family fortunes. Bess's father died young in 1527, leaving his only son, James, a minor less than two years old, so that the estate was taken into wardship for nearly twenty years. Once James inherited, he managed to lose heavily by foolish speculation, dying bankrupt in the Fleet Prison in London in 1581. A survey taken ten years earlier recorded that Hardwick Hall with the courts, barn yards and dovecote yard were valued at £2 per annum, the yearly value of the park was put at £65, and James's annual revenue was an estimated £341.

Feckless James was succeeded by his sister Bess. Never can there have been a more startling contrast between siblings. Where James was inept at management and foolish in speculation, Bess was a hard-headed businesswoman, wise in her investments, and tough in her bargains. Even so, she had a hard time raising the capital to buy Hardwick, complaining that her husband, the Earl of Shrewsbury, 'would not give her money to purchase the land of

Hardwick her brother deceased'. Nevertheless, on 2 June 1583, she bought Hardwick outright for £9,500 for her second, and favourite, son William Cavendish, acquiring also neighbouring Rowthorne and the Savage manors of Owlcotes, Stainsby and Heath for £3,416, so almost reuniting the parish of Ault Hucknall.

The best record of the Elizabethan estate is the volume of plans made for William Cavendish by William Senior, now preserved at Chatsworth House. Heath and Stainsby were surveyed in 1609; Astwith, Hardstoft, Hardwick and Rowthorne followed in 1610. Each village was drawn out on a separate sheet and the maps, each relating to a written survey, provide fascinating clues to the development of the settlements. Rowthorne and Stainsby then, as now, were built along a main street with crofts and tofts on either side. Hardstoft and Astwith, on the other hand, were ranged along the edge of commons. Today these two villages are disorderly in their layout because the commons were enclosed, and the villages lost their focal points. All four villages had independent field systems, but Senior's maps show that enclosures were already taking place, especially in Hardstoft. Early enclosure was piecemeal, strips of ridge and furrow being taken in bit by bit. This was reflected in the sinuous shapes of the fields in the nineteenth century, and remains apparent to a much reduced extent today. Later geometric enclosures of the eighteenth and nineteenth centuries, having less regard for the lie of the land, form a marked contrast with their predecessors.

Two areas of Ault Hucknall parish are missing from Senior's maps. One of them is the hamlet of Ault Hucknall itself, together with the glebeland there and the adjoining lands given to Newstead Abbey in the Middle Ages. After the Dissolution of the Monasteries, these ex-monastic lands were granted to Francis Leake of Sutton Scarsdale, and they did not become the property of the Devonshires until 1744. The other omission concerns lands on the western edge of the parish, where the Devonshires were still making purchases into the twentieth century. Some of the woodland here once belonged to the Sitwells of Renishaw, who converted the wood into charcoal to fuel their ironworkings.

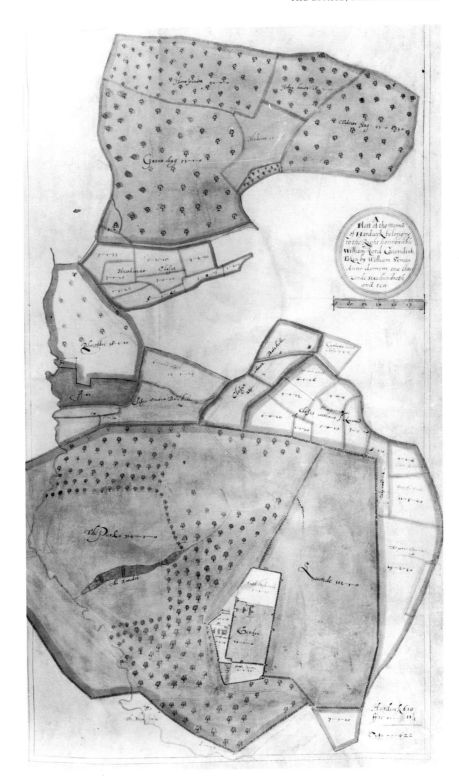

William Senior's map
of the estate at
Hardwick, 1610,
clearly showing the
park divided into two
parts

Hardwick stands out in Senior's plans as being quite different from the other parts of the parish. The park is boldly delineated and the manor is largely given over to woodland and pasture, with no village and no field system. Nothing is known of the park at Hardwick before James Hardwick's survey of 1570, although the evidence of deserted settlements and ridge and furrow suggests that it was not emparked until after the thirteenth century.

Senior's map shows the park divided into two, respecting the natural differences between its eastern and western parts. The western, larger part was typical of medieval parks, with tree-clothed banks intersected by watercourses. The hilly land there, overlying coal measures and lower Permian marl, was favoured by the oak trees for which Hardwick park was famous. Senior plotted the trees accurately, and they seem to have been grouped into well-defined areas, sometimes with distinct boundaries. This suggests careful planting or is possibly a reflection of earlier, now vanished, field boundaries.

The eastern part of the park overlies a limestone plateau on which ash grows best. The land here was called the 'lawnd' or lawn, signifying a flattish grassy area with a sparser tree cover. It was fenced off separately and was ploughed occasionally in the seventeenth century. Its topography rendered it the most suitable part of the park for a formal arrangement of trees, and in the seventeenth century an elm walk was planted there, probably in or around 1656. It does not appear to have been a success and was removed in 1730; the precise site of the elm walk is not known, but the present lime avenue possibly occupies the same ground.

In the second half of the seventeenth century, the park trees were maintained by the sowing and transplanting of oak, ash, elm and sycamore. Charcoal was made in the park around 1600, but there is no evidence that Hardwick timber was used to build either the Old or New Halls. The park was principally a deer reserve, although the deer shared the grazing with 'joist' cattle. 'Joist' cattle were animals belonging to local people who paid a fee to graze them in the park, a practice which only ceased in the present century. Closes to the north and east of the park were used for haymaking and the cultivation of wheat and oats. The woodland north of the park was divided into sections systematically managed, called 'hags'; this area is now known as Hucknall Wood.

By the 1630s, two large ponds had been dug in the western part of the park. They are not shown on Senior's plan, but they were later sketched in roughly in pencil, as though the plan was used to consider their excavation. In the seventeenth century, they were usually referred to as the Upper and Nether Great Ponds, and both of them supplied power to waterwheels. By 1712, Nether Pond was used as a reserve for Stainsby Mill, and eventually became known as Miller's Pond. In the second half of the seventeenth century, Upper Pond was used to drain the coalpits between the two ponds. The coal here lay immediately below the surface and was relatively easy to get out, but the workings tended to be waterlogged.

Determined efforts to mine coal in the park can be traced to 1656, when 4s 6d was spent 'about the intended engin in the park'. The 'engin' was a pump driven by a waterwheel, which was in turn driven by water from the Upper Great Pond. The whole apparatus came to be known as the 'gin', giving its name to nearby 'Gin Gate' (now obsolete). After several initial setbacks and near-disasters, mining was proceeding smoothly by the mid 1660s, but the venture was short-lived. After about 1672, the mines in the park fell into disuse, in favour of coal mines at Hardstoft.

In 1665 the park was greatly expanded by the addition of part of Rowthorne Carr and by the purchase from the Molyneux family of some emparked land in the neighbouring parish of Teversall. This land, consisting of banks of old trees, fish ponds, woodland pasture and a small deer park, was known as 'New Parke'.

By this period, however, the Cavendishes had come to prefer Chatsworth, and expenditure on Hardwick was meagre in comparison. The rebuilding of Chatsworth by the 1st Duke and the lavish layout of its gardens and park put Hardwick even further into the shade. The Old Hall became superfluous and in 1747–57 the eastern part was demolished. The south elevation, however, was saved, possibly for its picturesque effect. By now, the Romantic movement and the search for the

With the search for the Picturesque in the eighteenth century, the two Halls at Hardwick, so long neglected as outmoded and old fashioned, came back into their own. (*Above*) S.H. Grimm's reconstruction of the Hill Great Chamber in the Old Hall drawn in 1785. (*Below*) a romantic view of the ruins of the Old Hall by William Hunt, 1828

Picturesque, especially in landscape, were much in vogue. Sir John Vanbrugh had pleaded with Sarah, Duchess of Marlborough, for parts of the ruin of the medieval palace of Woodstock to be saved for the landscape garden at Blenheim, but in vain. The Cavendishes were wiser: the south front of Hardwick Old Hall was the subject of an engraving reproduced in the *European Magazine* in 1799, and the fine Elizabethan plasterwork still clings to the walls with great effect. The west end of the Old Hall was abandoned in 1789 or soon afterwards, but it somehow remained intact until the late nineteenth century.

By the end of the eighteenth century, the Baroque glories of Chatsworth seemed *passé*, and the Cavendishes showed renewed interest in Hardwick. One of the family, staying at Hardwick in February 1781, described it thus: 'The grounds of this place are beautiful, if it was the family seat and worth while, it might be made the finest place in England the hills are so bold, and so softened with wood, so romantick and wild, and with a very little trouble the water in the Valley might become an immense river.'

In 1790, the bells of Ault Hucknall rang to celebrate the birth of the future 6th Duke; an appropriate gesture, for William Spencer, known to posterity as the Bachelor Duke, was to have a special affinity with Hardwick. His *Handbook*, published in 1845, describes in detail the enormous amount of work he did at the Hall, but he also carried out some important changes in the park. In 1822–24 he made new drives through the park to Glapwell Gate and Blingsby Gate. These drives were bordered by 'clump avenues' of oak trees, normally called the 'Platoons' because of their likeness to groups of soldiers. In 1833, elaborate flower beds were laid out in the West Courtyard of the Hall and in 1844 Lady Spencer's Wood was extended by the addition of a yew walk. Some time before 1855, bare areas in the park were filled with a group of small circular and oval plantations.

In the years immediately following the 6th Duke's death in 1858, several ambitious improvements took place at Hardwick. Thomas Crump of Derby was commissioned in 1859 to install a steam engine to pump water up to the house and offices;

the engine house, with a detached, tall stone chimney, still survives in the park. The stables were completely overhauled and a new servants' wing was built at the north end of the Hall. Work of an equally extensive nature took place at the Great Ponds, which were remodelled and cleaned in 1857–61. This work necessarily damaged the natural marshy habitat for wildfowl, so in 1860 a duck decoy was built to compensate for the loss.

Of about two hundred decoys that have been constructed in England at one time or another, only about nine were cage decoys of the Hardwick type, and the Hardwick example was among the most perfect. The decoy was placed in the course of the River Doe Lea, and took the form of an elliptical island encircled by water. The whole was surrounded by a bank, in which two sight huts of stone and brick were built opposite each other, to the south-west and north-east of the island. There was a bridge with a handrail, built of thirteen oak posts and boarded with deal, to cross from the north-east hut to the island. The cage itself was made of iron, wood and wire. It had two compartments, and the trap doors at each end were operated by a system of pulleys, slides and wires. The decoy birds were always fed inside the cages, and plenty of food was left to tempt the wild birds to enter. Both trap doors were left up, and as soon as the decoyman observed any wild birds in either partition, he slowly lowered the door to entrap the birds. The captives were not taken out till after 'flighting' time.

The rural depression of late Victorian times spelt the end of decoys, and the one at Hardwick had fallen into disuse by the end of the century. One of the sight huts has recently been restored, but the decoy superstructure has disappeared and the site has reverted to a rather overgrown and marshy condition.

The extensive work at the Hall, in the park, and on the estate generally, was mirrored in the growth of the estate buildings on the hillside below the Stableyard, near Crump's Engine House. A sawmill was built there in 1861, and a new mason's shed, lime house and mess room were built in 1879. But by the 1870s the pace of developments was slowing down; Carr Plantation was planted in 1870, and Norwood Lodge was built in 1874, but the proposed lodges at Blingsby Gate and Gin Gate were never built. Life at Hardwick appears to have become uneventful, but the park was probably at its best in the 1870s and there was little substantial change until the First World War.

The economic difficulties brought about by the First World War meant reduction rather than improvement. The gardens could no longer be cultivated to the same extent, Lady Spencer's Walk was neglected and the flower beds in the West Court were turfed over.

In the park, the number of deer had fallen from 200 in 1892 to about 50 in 1920, and the animals were gradually phased out. The 'joist' cattle, a feature of Hardwick life for centuries, were also becoming a thing of the past. Every summer the local people would brand their cattle and bring them into the park to graze on 1 May: in the 1920s the rates were 25 shillings per cow for a tenant, 30 shillings for a non-tenant; 2 guineas per horse for a tenant, 50 shillings for a non-tenant. But by the early 1930s it had ceased to be a going concern; farmers had fewer cattle and their own grass. A suggestion that sheep should be grazed instead was considered unsatisfactory, so the Duke built up his own herd, and much of the former grassland in the eastern part of the park was put under the plough.

Timber shortage was another problem. The best timber had been removed in the First World War and by 1932 the leavings were almost exhausted. Recourse was made to hedgerow trees, although railway sleepers or concrete were used wherever possible. The park fence, traditionally maintained using riven timber, had now to be repaired with imported sawn timber and is today almost entirely of sawn wood.

Nevertheless, the lime avenue was planted in 1926–27, possibly on the site of the seventeenth-century elm walk. Because of its shape it is known as the Wine Glass. Over half a mile long, the avenue makes good use of the terrain and available space to obtain the best possible effect. It was the idea of Evelyn, wife of the 9th Duke of Devonshire, who was passionately interested in the trees at Hardwick.

At the outbreak of the Second World War, parts of the park were given over to the army and the RAF. The 1st Parachute Brigade was formed at Hardwick in 1941. For the remainder of the war Hardwick was the depot and School of Airborne Forces, where volunteers from all ranks of the Army went through selection tests and received their specialised training. Every airborne participant in the Normandy invasion, whether by parachute or glider, went through initial training at Hardwick. A bronze memorial plaque has recently been erected near the south-west corner of the car park in the North Orchard.

After the war the Army huts on the lower slopes of the park were used as a miners' hostel for the nearby open-cast strip coal mining. This land has now been reinstated for farming and can be seen on the far side of the M1 motorway. The camp was demolished in 1959 and nothing now remains except some of the roadways. However, when Millers Pond was dredged in the 1970s some 600 bicycles were recovered from the silt. They were dumped there out of sight having been commandeered by the troops on nights out in nearby towns after they had missed the transport back to camp.

The land on top of the limestone ridge was requisitioned by the RAF for a landing strip, and the resulting destruction is described by Evelyn, Duchess of Devonshire: 'I was very proud of a mile long avenue of limes planted 17 years ago and growing very well, but a great deal of it has been torn up to prepare for a landing place for aeroplanes. An opening was also made through a belt of trees planted perhaps 100 years ago to hide a colliery. Before the work was done the site was condemned as being quite unsuitable for landings, but that did not give us back our trees.' These missing trees were replaced soon after the end of the war, and are still noticeably smaller than the rest, but now, forty years on, the visual impact of the avenue is no longer seriously affected.

In 1959 Hardwick Hall came to the National Trust with 1,000 acres of adjacent park and woodland. Under the Countryside Act of 1968, the western part of the park was converted into a Country Park during the 1970s, allowing the clearing and restoration of the Great and Row ponds, the provision of footpaths, facilities for angling, and the building of a modest visitor information centre.

When the Trust took over Hardwick, it found that the park had been badly damaged by the dairy farming, so it seemed sensible to stock it with animals appropriate to the area, interesting to look at, and which would contribute to the preservation of breeds in danger of extinction. Choice was not difficult: longhorn cattle which once dominated the rural scene had not originated in the Midlands, but had been developed there two hundred years ago by the great breeder, Robert Bakewell, thirty miles away in Leicestershire. In addition a breed of sheep, White Faced Woodland, from the Peak District estates of the Devonshires was introduced.

HARDWICK INN

This building, situated at one of the southern park entrances, was built in 1608. It replaced an earlier inn on the same site, kept in the 1570s by a husbandman called Robert Tomson, who died in 1581. Tomson had been one of James Hardwick's tenants, paying an annual rent of 8 shillings for a 'tenement at the park gate' and certain land in Hardstoft. He was not a prosperous man; the inn supplemented his income as a farmer and was probably a poor establishment.

The present inn was built by John Ballechouse, known as John Painter, who figures prominently among the craftsmen working on the New Hall (see page 20). The accounts suggest that he was held in sufficiently high regard to work on his own initiative, and that he built and designed the inn for his own residence. The house was originally T-shaped, impressive and spacious.

John was succeeded by his son James, who served as 'receiver' for the estate. An inventory made in February 1647/48 provides a fascinating insight into the appearance of the inn.

It was expected that it would be furnished with 'Bedding furniture etc., fitting for the entertainment of gentlemen and strangers', and it was certainly comfortable by the standards of the time. It was taxed for 8 hearths in 1662, it had 6 chimneys and some of the walls were built very thick to accommodate spacious fireplaces. The Dining Par-

Hardwick Inn, built in the late sixteenth century by John Bellechouse, one of the leading craftsmen employed by Bess at Hardwick

lour, having a long table with a side form, 15 covered stools and 6 other seats, was designed to take a lot of people. It was made more relaxing by cushions, carpets, curtains, a glass lantern and '3 great pictures'. The Hall, more spartanly furnished with trestles, forms and stools, was evidently the bar. There was a brewhouse at the inn with a mash vat, and down in the cellars were a great brewing vat, 6 hogsheads, barrels and 'other wooden ware'. Upstairs, there were 8 chambers, the kitchen chamber being lavishly and extravagantly decked out in blue, yellow and black fabrics.

Books at the inn in 1648 included popular literature such as 'Smith's Sermons', 'ye practice of pietie', 'the book of Martiers [Foxe]', and a Bible.

Throughout the seventeenth and eighteenth centuries, upper servants from the Hall lived at the inn. It was restored and re-roofed in 1852–53, and possibly partially rebuilt.

STABLEYARD BUILDINGS

On the brink of a steep slope forming the edge of the limestone plateau stands the west range, consisting of brewhouse, wash house and dairy, built between 1589 and 1591. Brewing continued until 1857, and the brewhouse was converted into a house for the gardener in 1872. Today, most of the west range is occupied as staff accommodation.

Senior's plan of 1610 shows no buildings on the south side apart from a smithy, which still stands. By the mid seventeenth century it was joined by a slated great barn, which in this century was divided into a fire-engine shed, garages and a cowshed. The original form is nevertheless still discernible: open end to end, roof to floor with a threshing floor in the middle flanked by large doors.

In 1858–61 the stableyard buildings were repaired and altered, with the addition of a wagon-shed, and a clock and bell turret erected on the great barn.

HARDWICK GRANGE

A double pile house first built in the seventeenth century. Although its name suggests it was originally used as the grange for a monastery, this name dates only from Victorian times. In the seventeenth century it was known as Bolehill House, which gives the clue to its original use. Lead smelting hearths and ironstone smelting sites were known as bloomeries, or boles, and an earthwork immediately south of the Grange would be ideal for a bole, set into a bank on a high and windy west-facing hilltop. Prevailing winds from the west would have provided adequate blast, and trees from the park could have supplied fuel. There are references in the Hardwick muniments to 'blome-smythes' at Hardwick in the sixteenth century, so the Grange could well have been connected with the bloomery. Alternatively, it could have been a park keeper's lodge.

In 1724, however, the 2nd Duke turned the house into a school, giving a grant of £20 per annum: the southern part dates from this period, with an eastern gable of fine ashlar and bevelled quoins, and a datestone of 1724. The school continued until 1858, when a new building was provided at Hardstoft. The Grange is now a private house and is not open to the public.

STAINSBY MILL

There has been a watermill at Stainsby since the thirteenth century, probably on the same site as the present one, which is shown on Senior's plan of 1609. It passed to Bess of Hardwick with her purchase of the manor of Stainsby in 1593, and from the mid seventeenth century until its closure in the 1940s it was worked as part of Stainsby Mill Farm.

The mill dam at Stainsby was insufficient to power the mill: additional water was obtained from Millers Pond in Hardwick Park, and from Stainsby Pond, which was built in 1762 solely for the purpose of supplying the mill with water.

Following a period of disrepair in the 1840s, the building was completely reconstructed in 1849–50, and fitted with new machinery supplied by Kirkland & Son of Mansfield. The machinery is still remarkably complete and includes a kiln, drying floor, three pairs of stones and an iron waterwheel 5 feet wide and 17 feet in diameter. The mill was partially repaired by the National Trust in 1976, but further work is necessary before the building can be made accessible to the public.

THE GARDENS

The arrangement of courts and orchards around the New Hall is contemporary with the building of the house, and they form an integral part of the design. Like the house, they are symmetrical, apart from the truncation of the North Orchard due to the lie of the land. Although the grounds are spacious – 11 acres in all – they were never elaborate and have not always been meticulously kept.

In the mid seventeenth century, the gardener was 'old John Booth' who came over from Edensor armed with spade, rake and hoe to maintain the fruit and vegetables in the kitchen garden. Although he was not resident, he had several labourers at his command, including a local housewife to do the weeding. Apart from the kitchen garden, however, the other plots were sometimes wild and unkempt, with the grass grown long for hay, giving the Hall a rustic look.

In the 1660s a more ornamental approach was taken, with the elm walk planted in the 'Laund', 'a gravell walk in Hardwick garden for my lady to walke out on' replacing a turf alley, and fruit trees

planted in the West Court. But expenditure was deliberately kept low, as the Cavendishes were spending most of their money and their energies on the refurbishment of the house and garden at Chatsworth.

The outlines of the present gardens are still dictated by the seventeenth-century layout, but it was the developments of the nineteenth and early twentieth centuries that gave its present character.

The garden contains something of interest throughout the year. Spring bulbs and fruit blossom are followed by roses in the East Court and New Orchard and summer flowers in the long South Orchard border. The Herb Garden is at its best throughout the summer, while the West Court borders are most colourful in late summer and autumn.

WEST COURT

The original layout was simple, with paving down the centre. Fruit trees were planted in 1669, and subsequent references to pruning and nailing suggest they were trained up the walls: there is still a

The West Court borders are planted for late summer and autumn display using a graded colour scheme typical of the designs of Gertrude Jekyll. A proportion of tender plants bedded out each year is included for extra brilliance and length of flowering. Near the house, the colours are of rich purple, passing through red, orange and yellow, through to blue at the end furthest from the house, leavened by some white flowers such as the bottlebrushes of *Cimicifuga racemosa*

In the Herb Garden columns of Golden Hops *Humulus lupulus aureus* provide vertical accents in a formal planting of culinary and medicinal herbs, including the sweetly scented tobacco, *Nicotiana affinis*, Jackman's Blue Rue and an edging of chives

Created in the 1960s, the Herb Garden is the largest in any National Trust garden. Again edged by rue and chives, here can be seen the feathery leaves of fennel in front of French Sorrel and the dying autumn stems of Orach, saved for seed for the next year's crop

pear tree trained up the gatehouse. In 1833, the court was laid out as an elaborate flower garden by Blanche, the 6th Duke's niece, with a design centred on two beds in the shape of an E and an S, echoing Bess's initials on the parapets of the house, surrounded by circular beds, scrolls and borders. Plants originally included dahlias, lilac, laurel, roses, rhododendrons, heather and brooms. All this was swept away after the First World War and the court was turfed over. But in very dry weather the outlines of the beds can still be made out.

The only survivals from the nineteenth century are two cedars of Lebanon, planted as seedlings from 6-inch pots in the 1830s by the then Head Gardener, George Holmes.

The borders are planted in rich colours, using the sort of graded colour scheme favoured by Gertrude Jekyll.

EAST COURT

The East Court with its four yews was until recently plain green, a prelude to a view out over the ha-ha to the avenue of limes starting in an amphitheatre across the park, planted in 1930. The piers of the gateways, with bold capitals, plinths and scroll ornaments, probably date from 1686. The pond in the centre was made in 1920 as a fire-fighting reservoir but the Chesterfield fire-engine would have sunk before reaching the pool: the dilemma

The gatehouse with its elaborate strapwork cresting

was solved by laying a hard path under the turf. The green was enlivened by the introduction, in about 1950, of old roses that would tolerate the shade of the trees on one side and the northerly aspect on the other, with an underplanting of ground-cover plants such as bergenias and pulmonarias.

NORTH ORCHARD AND COURTYARD

This area always had a strong utilitarian purpose and although probably originally planted as an orchard seems never to have been neatly gardened. Thus in the 1650s there was a shed here for timber; in the 1870s a pheasantry. Sometimes it was opened up for 'joist' cattle. Now it is used as a car park.

SOUTH ORCHARD

In the seventeenth century, this area was planted with fruit trees, and was probably also the site of the kitchen garden, as it was until the present century. Today, it is divided into four quarters by hedged alleys of yew and hornbeam. This layout was devised by Lady Louisa Egerton, daughter of the 7th Duke, in 1861, incorporating lead statues brought over from Chatsworth.

The herb garden created by the National Trust in the 1960s occupies the south-western quarter. The plants are predominantly those that would have been familiar to an Elizabethan household. Next to it is a nuttery with walnuts, cobs and filberts, underplanted with naturalised spring flowers.

The two eastern quarters are occupied by orchards. The more formal, productive one to the south (the New Orchard) is planted with old varieties of apples, pears, plums, gages and damsons and has a border of old roses, clematis and tulips in the spring planted against a backcloth of the yew hedge. The second orchard, next to the house, has pears and ornamental crab apples more spaciously planted and in spring and early summer is treated as a wild garden, with mown paths through long grass containing naturalised bulbs.

The character of the north-west quarter, in contrast to both orchards and herb garden, is of a broad expanse of green lawn planted informally with specimen trees. There are several *Magnolia ×* *soulangiana* on the hedge side.

The sunny south-facing border in front of the

wall that divides the south garden from the entrance court contains herbaceous plants, including Hardwick's distinctive type of lily-of-the-valley, shrubs and old roses. Beyond the house, the predominantly herbaceous character gives way to billowing shrubs such as philadelphus, escallonias, buddleias, tree peonies and old roses, including 'Cerise Bouquet'.

Beyond the herb garden are nursery plots for growing cut flowers for the house and vegetables and a mulberry walk planted by the National Trust. At its southern end is one of the banqueting houses referred to on page 36. On occasion it was used by the 6th Duke's private orchestra as a smoking room since they were not allowed to smoke in the house.

LADY SPENCER'S WALK

On 22 December 1797, Harriet Cavendish, the twelve-year-old daughter of the 5th Duke, wrote to her governess from Hardwick: 'A thousand thanks, my dearest Selina, for your letters and the books. I have already begun the advantages of education. . . . I could not help smiling at one thing Maria had been amusing herself with, cutting a walk through a plantation, and yesterday my grandmama and I had been employed all the morning in the same thing.

We have entirely finished cutting it, and you cannot think how pretty it will be when it is covered with gravel.'

'Grandmama' was Georgiana, Countess Spencer, Harriet's maternal grandmother. The walk she made with her granddaughter's help was duly gravelled, and eventually the whole wood came to bear her name.

Originally, the walk consisted of a path through the middle of the plantation with a loop at each end. Some time in the early nineteenth century, the walk was extended further east to a small valley known as Hollowdale and later, in 1844, into Hollowdale itself.

Ornamental walks enclosed within parkland were not uncommon features in the later eighteenth century and were often embellished by flowering shrubs and trees such as lilacs, philadelphus, roses and laburnums.

The weeding and general maintenance of the walk was kept up until the First World War, but since then the wood has gradually returned to an uncultivated state, with the gravel walks becoming earth tracks. Nevertheless, it is an attractive wood and an important feature of the landscape.

The two orchard quarters occupying the east half of the South Garden are planted with traditional varieties of apple and pear, including Apple 'Duke of Devonshire'

BIBLIOGRAPHY

G. R. Batho, *Calendar of Talbot Papers in the College of Arms*, Derby, 1971

May H. Beattie, 'Antique Rugs at Hardwick Hall', *Oriental Art*, vol. V, no. 22, 1959

Francis Bickley, *The Cavendish Family*, London 1911

E. G. W. Bill, *Calendar of Shrewsbury Papers in Lambeth Palace Library*, Derby, 1966

David Bostick, 'Plaster Puzzle Decoded', *Country Life*, 26 July 1990

Lindsay Boynton, and Peter Thornton, 'The Hardwick Hall Inventories of 1601', *Journal of the Furniture History Society*, vol. VII, 1971

Margaret Cavendish, Duchess of Newcastle, *Autobiography* and *Life of William Cavendish, Duke of Newcastle*, reprinted London 1872

William George Spencer Cavendish, 6th Duke of Devonshire, *Handbook to Chatsworth and Hardwick*, privately printed, 1845

David N. Durant, *Bess of Hardwick*, London, 1977; revised edition, Newark, 1988

David N. Durant, *Arabella Stuart*, London, 1978

David N. Durant, and Philip Riden (eds), *The Buildings of Hardwick Hall*, Derbyshire Record Society, vols IV and IX, 1980 and 1984

Mark Girouard, *Robert Smythson and the Elizabethan Country House*, New Haven and London, 1983

Mark Girouard, 'Elizabethan Chatsworth', *Country Life*, 22 November, 1973

Lord Hawkesbury, 'Catalogue of the Pictures at Hardwick Hall, with a short account of the Heraldry in the various rooms', *Derbyshire Archaeological Society Journal*, vol. XXV, 1903

Joseph Hunter, *Hallamshire: History and Topography of the Parish of Sheffield*, Sheffield, 1819 and 1869

Christopher Hussey, 'Hardwick Hall', *Country Life*, 8, 15, 22 and 29 December, 1928

Margaret Jourdain, 'Needlework at Hardwick Hall', *Country Life*, 26 February, 1927; 'Some Tapestries at Hardwick Hall', *Country Life*, 26 March, 1927

Rev. Charles Kerry, 'Derbyshire Tapestry', in *Derbyshire Archaeological Society Journal*, 1894

Alastair Laing, 'Rechristenings at Hardwick', Country Life, 9 March 1989, pp. 134–5

Santina M. Levey, *The Hardwick Embroideries*, Worksop, 1988

Rosamund Meredith, *Catalogue of Arundel Castle MSS in Sheffield City Library*, Sheffield, 1965

John Nevinson, 'An Elizabethan Herbarium; Embroideries of Bess Hardwick after the Woodcuts of Mattioli', *National Trust Yearbook*, 1975–76

John Nevinson, 'Embroideries at Hardwick Hall' *Country Life*, 29 November, 1973

P. F. Robinson, *New Vitruvius Britannicus*, London 1835

Marcel Roethlisberger, 'The Ulysses Tapestries at Hardwick Hall', *Gazette des Beaux-Arts*, February, 1972

J. de Serre, 'Furniture at Hardwick Hall', *Country Life*, 23 April, 1927

Basil Stallybrass, 'Bess of Hardwick's Buildings and Building Accounts', *Archaeologia*, vol. LXIV, 1913

Margaret Swain, *The Needlework of Mary, Queen of Scots*, New York, 1973

George Wingfield Digby, *Elizabethan Embroidery*, London, 1963

INDEX